D1294208

HAND WEAVING
and Cloth Design

HAND WEAVING
and Cloth Design

Marianne Straub

A Studio Book
The Viking Press
New York

Published in 1977 by the Viking Press
625 Madison Avenue, New York, N.Y. 10022

This book was designed and produced by
George Rainbird Limited
36 Park Street, London W1Y 4DE

House Editor: Felicity Luard
Designer: Pauline Harrison
Index by: Susan Piquemal

Printed and bound in Great Britain

Frontispiece and title page:
Score, designed on a hand loom for
Tamesa Fabrics by Marianne Straub. Photo:
Architectural Review

Library of Congress Cataloging in Publication Data
Straub, Marianne.
    Hand weaving and cloth design.
    (A Studio book)
    Bibliography: p.
    Includes index.
    1. Hand weaving.   2. Textile design.   I. Title.
TT848.S75   746.1′4   76–16558
ISBN 0–670–36037–6

Contents

Glossary of terms

Apron Strong canvas cloth, tacked to the warp and cloth beams, to hold the warp.

Apron stick Flat stick, placed in the apron hem, to which the portee and starting sticks are tied.

Back bar A bar fixed at the back of the loom to guide the warp forward.

Backed cloth Single cloth strengthened or weighted by extra ends or picks.

Balanced cloth A square-set cloth.

Batten (beater, sley) A swinging frame used to beat in the weft. It holds the reed and supports the passage of the shuttle. Overslung: suspended from the top of the loom; underslung: pivoted at the base.

Beam (roller) The warp (back) beam carries the warp at the back of the loom, the cloth beam carries the woven cloth at the front.

Beaming Winding the warp on to the warp beam.

Bobbin Carries the weft yarn in the shuttle.

Breast bar (front bar) A bar fixed at the front of the loom to guide the cloth on to the cloth beam.

Cone Conical free-standing yarn package.

Cop Cylindrical yarn package requiring a supporting spindle.

Counterbalanced loom The shafts balance each other and form a centre shed.

Countermarch loom The shafts are balanced separately by lams and pedals and move in opposing directions.

Cramming Increasing the number of ends or picks over a limited area.

Cross sticks (lease rods or sticks) A pair of round rods or flat sticks inserted in the warp to retain the lease cross.

Cut Term for a unit length of Galashiels woollen yarn.

Denier Unit weight in grammes of continuous filament yarn.

Dents The spaces between the reed wires.

Dobby Mechanism to raise the shafts of a dobby loom according to a pattern chain of pegged lags.

Doup Half heddle used for gauze/leno weaving.

Draft The order in which the ends are threaded in the shafts.

Dressing the loom (looming) Preparing the warp in the loom preparatory to weaving.

Easer bar A cross bar which relaxes the warp tension intermittently as required.

End Single warp thread, runs through the length of the cloth.

Entering Threading the warp through heddles/healds and reed.

Fan reed (ondulé reed) Special reed with groups of wires converging in alternate fan shapes; produces a distorted warp.

Fancy yarn (novelty yarn) Textured yarns produced by special spinning or doubling processes.

Fell The edge of the cloth that faces the reed during weaving, where the last pick has been beaten up.

Felting Interlocking or matting of fibres caused by milling the cloth.

Fibres Single units that make up a thread. Categorized as animal, vegetable, mineral or synthetic; they vary greatly in length.

Filament Continuous thread. There are multifilament and monofilament yarns.

Finishing Various cloth treatment processes to improve the appearance and handle after removal from the loom.

Float Warp or weft thread that stretches across more than two ends or picks between intersections.

Fly shuttle Shuttle set in motion mechanically.

Folded yarn (doubled, plied) Yarn composed of two or more single threads twisted together.

Grey cloth Unfinished cloth.

Ground cloth Basic cloth which supports extra ends and/or picks.

Handle Term used to describe the feel of a cloth.

Heading Picks of a different yarn or colour woven in plain weave at the beginning of a cloth to show up mistakes in threading and reeding.

Heald Twisted galvanized wire or stamped narrow stainless steel strip with an eye in the centre to carry a warp end.

Heald frame Industrial-type frame shafts carrying wire or steel healds.

Heddle Looped cord of varnished string with an eye in the centre through which a warp end is threaded in the shafts.

Horizontal warping mill (sectional warping mill) Large horizontal reel used to make the warp in sections. May be turned by hand or motor.

Jack loom Pedal loom with a rising shed, available in the U.S.A.

Jacks Centrally pivoted levers on countermarch loom.

Lags Wooden slats carrying pegs, used in the dobby mechanism to control the rising of the shafts.

Lams Levers pivoted between shafts and pedals of a counterbalanced or countermarch loom to centralize the shedding action.

Lea Term for linen count used in the fixed weight system.

Lease cross The ends are retained in their correct sequence by crossing each other between a pair of pegs or cords (horizontal warping mill) during warping.

Lease reed Coarse reed with alternate dents closed to form a hole, used to separate the ends for the cross formation.

Lifting plan Order of raising the shafts for a dobby or table loom.

Loom Device to hold the warp taut during weaving.

Milling The application of friction and pressure to a cloth in hot soapy water, after scouring, to cause shrinking and felting, giving a compact fibrous surface.

Pawl Metal tongue that engages with a ratchet wheel to control the rotation of the beam.

Pedal tie-up Order in which the pedals are tied to the lams.

Pedalling order Sequence of pressing down the pedals.

Pedals (treadles) Pivoted, foot-operated levers that activate the shafts via the lams.

Pick (filling) Single weft thread woven across the width of the warp.

Picking Operation of passing the shuttle from one side of the shed to the other.

Picking plan Order in which the shuttles are brought into action.

Pirn Narrow cylindrical weft package.

Ply To twist two or more single threads together.

Point paper (graph paper) Design paper ruled in squares with bar lines enclosing groups of eight. Used for weave and draft notation.

Portee A group of warp threads run together on a vertical warping mill or warping board.

Portee cross (raddle cross) Crossing formed by placing alternate portees over and under, and under and over a pair of pegs on the warping mill.

Portee stick Used to attach the beginning of the warp to the apron stick.

Raddle Coarse reed with round wooden or metal pegs and removable top bar, used to spread warp to correct width during beaming.

Reed Evenly spaced metal wires held between baulks, used to divide the warp threads in the loom.

Reed marks Vertical lines running through the cloth, caused by the reed wires when too many ends are entered in each dent.

Reeding plan (reed notation, denting plan) Order of entering the ends in the reed when the spacing is irregular.

Scouring Washing a cloth in hot, soapy water to remove oil and dirt.

Section Group of warp threads run together on a horizontal warping mill.

Selvage The firmly woven edge of a cloth.

Sett (verb set) The number of ends and picks in a unit square of cloth.

Setting (crabbing) Steaming the cloth to stabilize the yarn contraction before washing.

Shaft (harness) A pair of flat sticks between which the heddles are stretched. Also a wood or metal frame holding metal healds.

Shed The opening formed between the ends through which the pick is inserted. Rising shed: ends raised from the neutral position. Sinking shed: ends lowered from the neutral position. Centre shed: all ends change position, some rising and some sinking.

Shuttle Implement used to carry the weft through the shed.

Shuttle box Box-shaped receptacle for the shuttle fixed at either end of the fly-shuttle batten.

Shuttle race Lower part of the batten in front of the reed which supports the passage of the shuttle.

Sleying Entering the ends in the reed.

Spool (bobbin) Cylindrical yarn package, rotates for yarn delivery used in warping.

Square-set Cloth with an identical warp and weft set at an equal density.

Staple Term used to denote length of fibre.

Stenter frame (tenter frame) Frame for drying washed cloth.

Stentering Drying a cloth at full width under controlled tension.

Stitching thread (binder) End or pick that stitches two cloth layers together.

Suction possing stick Stick fitted with a rubber suction pad at one end.

Swift (rice) Skein holder, hank holder.

Take-up Decrease in length of

warp and weft due to the curving of the yarn in the cloth.

Temple (template) Device to retain the cloth width during weaving.

Threading (drawing in) Pulling the warp ends through the heddle or heald eyes.

Twist direction The direction in which a yarn is spun or plied. Z twist: clockwise; S twist: anti-clockwise (counterclockwise).

Twist factor The number of twists per measured unit.

Vertical warping mill Large vertical reel for making the warp.

Wadding end/pick Thick end or pick used to increase the prominence of a rib.

Warp Threads running through the length of the cloth.

Warp-faced fabric A preponderance of warp over weft on the cloth face.

Warp pile Loops or cut loops formed by the warp.

Warp sticks Sticks inserted between layers of warp on the beam to keep the warp firm.

Warping Measuring and laying parallel the threads that will form the warp.

Warping board Pegged board for making the warp.

Warping plan The order in which the ends are placed on the warp beam if more than one colour or yarn type is used.

Weave notation Graphic representation of the warp and weft interlacing.

Weft (filling) The threads that run from selvage to selvage across the cloth.

Weft-faced fabric A preponderance of weft over warp on the cloth face.

Weft pile Loops or cut loops formed by the weft.

Yarn A continuous strand of twisted fibres.

Yarn count The size or thickness of the yarn.

Yarn creel (spool rack) Free-standing frame or rack that holds the yarn packages during warping.

Yarn packages See bobbin, cone, cop, pirn, spool.

Author's note

It has been my aim to make the weaver understand the basic principles of woven-cloth construction in order to give him/her the opportunity to apply a creative talent to the full and to use the available equipment to the best advantage. I believe that by thoroughly comprehending the methods by which weave constructions are evolved, the traditional theories of cloth design can constantly be reassessed in the light of a more adventurous attitude to fabrics and the availability of a changing range of yarns.

This book has been written for people who have learned to weave and have discovered that they have become involved in a craft that has many aspects and offers a seemingly endless chain of mutations concerning aesthetic and practical considerations. I hope that it will be of value to the seriously committed hand weaver, professional or amateur, and to those designers who use the hand loom for the weaving of initial trials and prototypes for industrial production.

To write a comprehensive treatise on weaving would require many volumes. It is essential that a book such as this should be kept within defined limits if it is to be of any practical assistance to the weaver wanting to gain the freedom to originate designs. I have chosen to confine this book to shaft-woven fabrics and weaving techniques that are based on the weft insertion by a shuttle. All forms of weaving that require finger manipulation have been excluded. Also excluded are all forms of pre-weaving patterning of warp and weft, such as warp printing, resist dyeing by tying etc.

Limited space has made it impossible to include a chapter on the mechanism and design scope of the Jacquard loom. To touch on the subject cursorily seems pointless; to cover it fully would require another book. However, I have discussed briefly the main differences between the hand and the power loom for the benefit of those who use the hand loom for the purpose of exploring new design ideas that can subsequently be industrially produced.

Although the basic system of the weaver's shorthand notation is generally accepted, there are minor variations in the layout and in the symbols used. It may require a moment's thought before my system becomes clear to those used to another form of layout. Equally, when discussing the weaver's tools, the warping equipment, looms and ancillary equipment, one is aware of the lack of a generally accepted terminology.

Acknowledgments

I am greatly indebted to Eileen Ellis for reading the manuscript and for her constructive criticism, to Wilfred Sandbach for correcting my manuscript and to Melissa Cornfeld for her advice on American terminology and methods. I would like to thank Kay Cosserat and Alison Howells for allowing me to include reproductions of their work, and I am also grateful to John Hunnex for the excellent colour photographs, and to the editor of *Crafts* magazine for allowing me to reproduce the photographs taken by Philip Sayer.

1 Designing and planning woven cloths

Weaving is a complex craft in which intuition must be related to planning. In cloth design, aesthetic and practical requirements cannot be considered independently. Every cloth has a practical purpose, and the designer/weaver must relate these considerations to functional demands. It is therefore essential to design with a specific purpose in mind. In fact, demands and limitations can often be a positive stimulus rather than a frustration, and by overcoming them the weaver develops an analytical as well as creative approach to design problems. The initial steps in learning to construct a cloth are best taken on the loom where the results can be seen and handled.

A cloth is woven from two sets of threads that cross each other at right angles. The warp threads (ends) run through the length of the cloth while the weft threads (picks) interlace across the warp to form a web. The pattern and quality of a fabric, its strength, abrasion resistance, handle, and other factors specific to a cloth's function, are determined by the colour and character of its yarns, the spacing of the warp and weft threads (the cloth density), and the way in which they are interlaced (the weave construction).

Whether the cloth is to be plain or highly decorative, the design process is constructional. However, the emphasis placed on different aspects may vary. Thus a plain cloth will emphasize the yarn quality, while a prominent pattern can disguise the fact that quality has taken second place to pattern effect.

Colour and texture, of course, are both important in cloth design, and their interplay can be infinitely varied. In weaving, colour relationships are similar to those in a *pointilliste* painting; thread intersections are equivalent to horizontal and vertical brush strokes. When the same colour is used for both warp and weft yarns, and their size and texture are identical, the pattern made by the thread intersections is often almost entirely subdued. Only changes of light reflection give some indication of the weave construction.

The use of different colours introduces a new design element: visual patterns can be created in the fabric that are quite distinct from those formed by the weave's construction. The extent to which coloured yarns make a visible pattern depends entirely on their distribution in the fabric, on the weave construction, and on the fineness of the cloth. For example, a square-set plain-weave cloth with a red warp and blue weft will be seen as a purple fabric if it is very fine but as a red and blue checkerboard when woven from very coarse yarns. And between these two extremes lies a whole range of subtle colour variations. By using the cloth construction, colour placing, and fineness of cloth in limitless combinations, the designer/weaver has the power to create an almost infinite spectrum of colours, shades, and tones.

Patterned cloths are pre-planned in a simple form. For example, a sketch – not concerned with details of texture or colour interactions – can be a useful guide in assessing the proportions of stripes, checks or patterns. Colour relationships in a striped weave can be explored with strips of cloth mounted on airmail paper (so that they can be cut and joined together in any order without fraying); or by winding dyed yarns on to stiff card, but bearing in mind the weave construction and density.

If there is no obvious design feature, it is not possible to interpret a cloth's effect graphically. And to try to do so would only be a waste of time. The designer must therefore learn to visualize a cloth mentally – to form a concept of the design as an abstract visual image and to develop it in the mind. The ability to translate the idea from a visual image into all the factors that play a part in designing comes with experience and an increasing knowledge of weave constructions.

It is essential to visualize the cloth as it will be used: for example, hanging at a window, covering a chair, or made up into a garment. By 'seeing' the cloth in context it is easier to determine its quality and pattern scale; and in this way the cloth's design is related directly to its function.

Though the initial concept of a cloth may have been sparked off by a specific cloth requirement or, for example, by a range of yarns or colours that set in motion a host of design ideas, no aspect of cloth design can be planned in isolation. The choice of yarn, the weave construction (see pages 65 to 141), the density of the cloth setting, the choice of reed and, in some cases, the finishing process (see page 142) are the main factors to consider.

CHOICE OF YARNS

The handle of a fabric, its draping potential and the texture are affected by the choice of yarn (see colour illustration on page 25). The nature of the fibre and the yarn texture affect both the light reflection and response to dyeing. For example, silk, a continuous filament yarn, has an unbroken surface and gives the brightest colour reflection.

SINGLE YARNS A single yarn is a continuous strand of twisted fibres. The strength, elasticity, and texture are determined by the character of the fibre and the method of spinning.

FOLDED (PLIED) YARNS These yarns consist of two, three or more yarns twisted together; the twist generally runs in the opposite direction to

(*opposite above*) The yarn twist can be used as an integral part of the cloth design. Here alternating bands of S- and Z-twisted weft yarn give an effective zigzag pattern to a plain weave construction.

(*opposite below*) As the yarn is wound on to a bobbin, the yarn from the upper cone winds round that from the lower cone forming a loosely plied yarn with a Z twist. An S twist is made when the yarn comes off the upper cone in the opposite direction.

Yarns are spun or folded in either direction. An 'S' twist follows the twist downward from left to right, a 'Z' twist from right to left, corresponding with the letters' main stroke. The angle of the twist is governed by the number of turns per measured unit. Here the Z-ply yarn is made from two S-spun threads, and the S-ply yarn from two Z-spun threads. Photo: John Hunnex

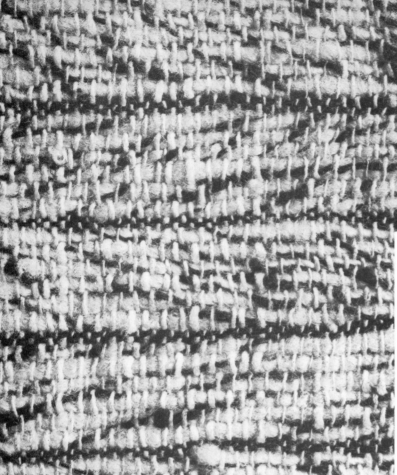

the twist of the component single yarns. Folded yarns are usually strong and smooth. When different colours are combined, the resultant folded yarn is called a 'marl' yarn. Redoubled folded yarns are known as 'cable' yarns.

To make your own, loosely plied yarn, place one cop or cone of yarn below another and run the thread of the lower yarn package cone through the centre of the upper cone (see illustration). As the yarn is wound on to a spool or bobbin, the thread of the upper cone will twist round the thread passing through its centre. Any yarn combination can be made in this way.

Man-made yarns (single or plied) in general lack texture interest. To extend their range of use and to make them more attractive and elastic, they

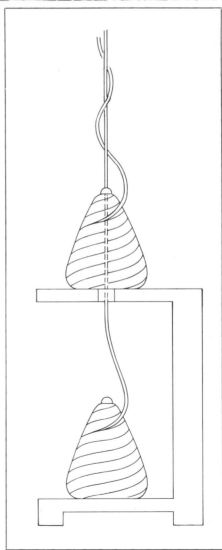

11

have been subjected to a mechanical texturing process.

FANCY YARNS These include all yarns that are spun and/or folded by more complex methods. Only some are suitable for the warp, but all can be used as weft. Few fancy yarns have only one component, most of them are formed with three components, some with two, and a few with more than three.

Single-component fancy yarns include 'knicker' (knickerbocker) and 'slub' yarns. In knicker yarns flecks of different colour or texture are incorporated into the yarn. Only if these are firmly embedded is the yarn suitable as warp. Slub yarns have stretches of alternating thick and thin places, preferably distributed at random. The twist accumulates in the fine sections of the yarn. The yarn can only be used in warps where the reed abrasion is kept to a minimum.

Two-component fancy yarns are made by doubling a coarse and a fine yarn. The fine yarn, being under greater tension, forms grooves in the coarser yarn. These spiral yarns are generally strong and suitable for warps.

Most fancy yarns are multi-component yarns, for example, *gimp*, *snarl*, *knop*, *loop*, *bouclé*, and *corkscrew* yarns. If they are to be used in the warp it is essential that the texture is not too prominent and that the binder yarn used to retain the 'fancy' effect is very strong.

Brushed yarns should be used only intermittently. If the cloth is to have a brushed appearance, a yarn suitable for brushing, such as a loop yarn, should be used and the cloth brushed during the finishing process (see page 142).

SPACE-DYED AND PRINTED YARNS Any yarn may be space-dyed by the ikat method, injection dyeing, dip-dyeing, printing, etc. (see colour illustration on page 127). The spacing of the colour areas can be infinitely varied. The result will be more or less brilliant according to the nature and texture of the yarn.

Warp yarns
The warp has to sustain considerable tension during weaving, and must withstand continuous friction caused by the movement of the shafts and the reed. Yarn for the warp should therefore be chosen for its strength, elasticity, and abrasion resistance.

Strength and elasticity are related: elasticity will compensate, to some extent, for deficiency in strength – an inelastic yarn tends to snap under tension. To test strength and elasticity, hold a piece of yarn about a metre long stretched out taut between the hands, and gradually increase the tension until it breaks. If the yarn breaks as soon as you apply any tension, then it is unsuitable for use in a warp. But repeat this test several times as a yarn may have occasional weak places.

Lack of abrasion resistance in a yarn is another major fault. Once loose fibres begin to appear and to cause the warp yarns to stick together, the effect is cumulative and almost impossible to put right. To test the abrasion resistance, hold the yarn stretched taut between the thumb and fingers of one hand, and with the thumbnail and ball of the first finger of the other, rub the exposed length backward and forward about twenty times. If loose fibres do not appear after repeating the test several times with a reasonable amount of pressure, then the yarn should present no difficulties in the loom.

If several different yarns are to be used in a warp, each one must be tested for strength and abrasion resistance.

Weft yarns
Weft yarns are not subject to either strain or abrasion. The size of the yarn is therefore the only thing that may make it unsuitable for use in a shuttle.

THE YARN COUNT
The yarn count expresses the thickness of the yarn, and must be known before calculating the quantity of yarns for a known length of fabric.

The yarn-count number indicates the length of the yarn in relation to the weight.

Three systems of yarn count are currently in use: the fixed-weight, the fixed-length, and the Tex systems. The fixed-weight system can be used with British and American weights and measures. The fixed-length system and the Tex system are based on metric weights and measures. Tex is an internationally agreed system of yarn numbering that applies to all types of yarns, regardless of the method of production.

The fixed-weight system

The fixed-weight yarn-count system is used for numbering spun yarns. It is based on the length of yarn per lb weight. The greater the length of yarn weighing 1 lb, the finer it is and the higher the count number. The count number gives the number of unit lengths i.e. skeins, hanks, etc. in 1 lb: for example, 10 hanks cotton (abbreviated to 10's cotton); 12 skeins Yorkshire woollen spun (12's Y.sk.).

The unit length of 1's count (i.e. one unit length to 1 lb weight) varies with different fibres and spinning systems:

Woollen spun	Galashiels	cut	200 yd
	Yorkshire	skein	256 yd
	West of		
	England	hank	320 yd
Worsted		hank	560 yd
Linen		lea	300 yd
Cotton		hank	840 yd
Spun silk		hank	840 yd

Man-made spun yarns are numbered according to their spinning method.

To find the length of a yarn of a known count, the unit length is multiplied by the count number. Example: 10's cotton has $10 \times 840 = 8400$ yd per lb.

When a yarn is plied, that is when two yarns of idential count are twisted together, the yarn is twice as thick and therefore the length of a lb weight is halved. The numbering of the yarn states both the count of the single component and the number of components that make up the ply. Example: 2/10's cotton; the length of this yarn would be $\frac{10 \times 840}{2} = 4200$ yd per lb. All plied yarns within the fixed-weight system state the number of components before the count of the yarn, with the exception of spun silk. In this case the yarn count precedes the number of components, 30/2 spun silk. In this example the count is 30 made up of two components each having a count of 60, giving a total yarn length of $30 \times 840 = 25,200$ yd per lb.

The fixed-length system

This system is used to number continuous filament yarns, i.e. reeled silk and man-made extruded yarns. It is based on a fixed yarn length to a variable weight, and is measured in deniers. The denier count of a yarn states the weight in grammes per 9000 metres. Thus a 10-denier yarn will weigh 10 grammes and measure 9000 metres. The coarser the yarn, the higher the denier count number becomes. Thus 9000 metres of a 30-denier yarn weigh 30 grammes.

The Tex system

The Tex system is also based on the fixed-length system, i.e. weight per unit length. The Tex count represents the weight in grammes per 1 kilometre (1000 metres) of yarn, i.e. a yarn numbered 10 Tex measures 1 kilometre and weighs 10 grammes. The Tex number increases with the size of the yarn.

The yarns are labelled according to an international code. The yarn count number is followed by the word Tex. The term 'folded' is used in preference to 'plied' yarn when two or more yarns are twisted together, and the direction of the twist is included in the information. Example: R 20 Tex/2 S; two threads of 10 Tex are folded in an 'S' direction, therefore the resultant count (R) will be 20 Tex because the weight is exactly doubled.

When the yarn count is not known, it can be established by measuring a length of 10, 50 or 100 metres depending on the count you judge the yarn to be. This is best done on a swift (a skein or hank holder) set to a circumference of 1 metre. The hank is then weighed in grammes; e.g. if 50 metres of yarn weigh 2 grammes, 1000 metres will weigh 40 grammes, and the count is therefore 40 Tex.

THE CLOTH SETTING

The number of ends and picks in a measured unit is called the 'setting' of the cloth. A distinction is made between 'warp sett', expressed as ends per centimetre or inch (e/cm or epi), and 'weft sett', expressed as picks per centimetre or inch (p/cm or ppi).

The setting of a cloth, or how closely the threads should lie together, depends on several inter-related factors:

1 The weave construction, i.e. the number of thread intersections there are within the repeat unit. (This also affects the degree of cloth contraction.)
2 The yarn count (the yarn size).
3 The character and texture of the yarn.
4 The practical purpose of the cloth.
5 Aesthetic considerations.
6 Whether or not the cloth will undergo a finishing process that causes shrinkage.

To decide the setting of a cloth, most hand weavers use an empirical method that bases the warp sett on the count of the yarn and the number of thread intersections within the weave repeat. (If the frequency of intersections varies – some picks regularly intersecting the warp and others mainly floating over it – it is usually the more firmly woven cloth that determines the density.)

When the warp and weft yarns are of identical count (size), the weft intersections will occupy the same space as the ends. Thus, if there are eight ends lying side by side in 1 cm (20 in 1 in) of a plain-weave cloth, the pick intersections between them will take up the same space again, spreading out the ends over 2 cm (2 in). To find the warp setting, wind the warp yarn round a ruler or stiff card, placing the threads carefully side by side over a distance of one or more centimetres (inches) depending on the thickness of the yarn. Count the number of threads over the measured area and add the number of weft intersections. The figure thus arrived at is the space required over which the warp has to be spaced.

If the weft is only half the count of the warp yarn, the weft intersections will require only half the space of the ends, i.e. two intersections count as one warp thread. If it is coarser than the warp yarn the weft intersections will take up more space than the ends.

The character of both warp and weft yarns also plays an important part in deciding the setting. The above practice of relating yarn diameter to thread intersection applies to smooth straight yarns. In general, the more texture a yarn has, the more open the setting can be. When a finishing process causing yarn shrinkage is involved (see page 142), make allowance in the setting for the degree of cloth contraction.

A more accurate mathematical formula can be used to calculate the setting of a cloth designed for a purpose that makes high demands on its performance. Again based on the diameter of the yarn and the relative yarn intersections, it also makes percentage adjustments for the yarn character and shrinkage.

WARP CALCULATIONS

Determining the number of ends

To calculate the number of ends in the warp, multiply the width of the warp by its sett, i.e. the number of ends per centimetre (e/cm) or inch (epi).

Example:
Width of warp: 110 cm (44 in) ⎫ $110 \times 6 = 660$
e/cm: 6 (15 epi) ⎭ ends in the warp

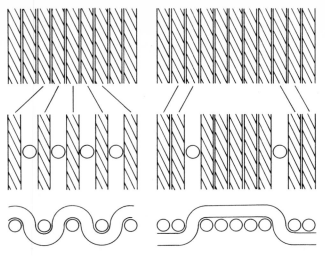

When the warp and weft yarns are of identical count (size), the weft intersections will occupy the same space as the ends.

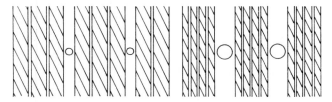

If the yarn counts differ, either less or more space must be allowed for the weft intersections.

If there are to be 20 ends in each portee, 660/20 portees will be needed to make up the warp, i.e. 33.

When deciding the warp width, it is important to remember that a certain amount of contraction takes place during weaving and that the final cloth width will depend on the character of the weave construction and the elasticity of the weft yarn, and on the finishing process.

If the reeding is irregular, that is if the warp ends are not evenly spaced in the reed (see page 27), then a different calculation is required. Divide the width of the warp by the width of the reeding-plan unit to find the number of repeats in the warp, and then multiply this figure by the number of ends in the reeding plan (see page 64).

Example :
Width of warp : 110 cm (44 in)
Reed : 32 dents per dm (8 dents per in)
Reeding plan : /3/3/1/3/1/1/0/0/3/0/0/1/1/3/1/3
   = 24 ends in 16 dents
Width of reeding-plan unit : 16 dents = 5 cm
   (2 in)
Number of reeding-plan units in the warp :
   110/5 = 22
Total number of ends in the warp : 22 × 24 = 528

Selvage ends are usually included in the width calculation if they are of the same yarn.

Calculating the length of the warp
When deciding the length of the warp, take account of the inches of warp that will be unavoidably wasted at the beginning and end of the cloth, and also of the cloth's contraction once it has been taken off the loom. To calculate this contraction, and hence the extra warp length required, cut a 20-cm (8-in) strip of the same or similar cloth, draw out a warp thread and measure it stretched taut. Work out the extra length (i.e. degree of contraction) as a percentage of 20 cm and add the same percentage to the length of the warp.

YARN QUANTITIES

To establish the quantity of yarn required for the warp that has been planned, the number of ends in the warp is multiplied by the length of each end, and divided by the length of the yarn.

The calculation based on the fixed-weight system:

Warp length: 10 yd
Warp width: 42 in
epi: 20 ends
Yarn: 12's cotton

$$\frac{\text{Warp length in yards} \times \text{warp width in inches} \times \text{ends per inch} \times \text{weight conversion into ounces}}{\text{yarn count} \times \text{unit length}} = \text{weight in ounces}$$

Represented in figures: $\dfrac{10 \times 42 \times 20 \times 16}{12 \times 840} = 13\frac{1}{3}$ oz

The calculation based on the Tex system:

Warp length: 9 m
Warp width: 115 cm
e/cm: 8 ends
Yarn: 50 Tex

$$\frac{\text{Warp length in metres} \times \text{warp width in centimetres} \times \text{ends per centimetre} \times \text{Tex count}}{\text{unit length}} = \text{weight in grammes}$$

Represented in figures: $\dfrac{9 \times 115 \times 8 \times 50}{1000} = 414$ g

When the warp contains yarns of various counts, each yarn quantity has to be calculated separately.

To calculate the quantity of yarn needed for the weft, multiply the length of the piece to be woven, the width of the warp and the picks per inch, and divide by the yarn's length.

The calculation based on the fixed-weight system:

$$\frac{\text{Woven length in yards} \times \text{warp width in inches} \times \text{picks per inch} \, (\times \text{ounces})}{\text{yarn count} \times \text{unit length}}$$

The calculation based on the Tex system:

$$\frac{\text{Woven length in metres} \times \text{warp width in centimetres} \times \text{picks per centimetre} \times \text{yarn count}}{\text{unit length}}$$

THE CHOICE OF REED

The reed should be chosen after consideration of its major functions, which are to separate the warp ends, to hold them parallel, and to beat the weft against the fell of the cloth. The choice should be based on the yarn character, the density of the warp sett, as well as on the requirements of the specific cloth construction. In addition there are two factors that must be taken into account, whatever the character of the yarn and the cloth construction may be:

1 The reed spacing must be sufficiently wide to permit the passage of a knotted yarn without undue friction. If a warp contains a variety of yarn counts, choose the reed spacing to accommodate the coarsest knotted end. Knotless yarns are available, at a price, for industrial production. A hand weaver can when necessary eliminate all knots during warping, although this does entail some wastage.

2 It is important to keep the friction caused by the reed to a minimum. For this reason, avoid putting a single end in a dent, as the reed wires then take up too much space and rub against the yarn. A warp with a very open sett is an exception to this rule.

On the other hand, when too many ends are entered in one dent, the cloth will show 'reed marks': vertical lines particularly noticeable in cotton, linen, and synthetic fabrics. Such lines usually disappear if a finishing process is used. However, they can be used as a design feature.

The reed movement assists shed formation considerably by separating out the ends. Hairy yarn, or any yarn that tends to stick together, should wherever possible be entered two in a dent only to avoid abrasion.

The choice of the reed is also important from the point of view of emphasizing certain design features of a cloth construction.

2 Hand looms

Floor and table looms are two main types of 'hand loom' used. The weaver uses both hands and feet to work a floor loom but operates the table loom by hand only. On the floor loom, therefore, the weaving process can become a rhythmical sequence of actions following each other in unbroken succession – pedal depression, shed opening, weft insertion, and beating up. Weaving on a table loom, however, is unrhythmical and therefore considerably slower.

There are two basic types of floor loom, the pedal and dobby. Within these categories looms are distinguished from each other by their shedding mechanism: the mechanism for raising the warp ends to form a shed. Because this mechanism determines the scope of a weave construction and may impose limitations on the length of the pattern repeat, it is the most important feature of a loom, followed only by the warp-tension control (see page 20).

Pedal looms are either counterbalanced (page 28) or countermarch (page 30) looms. Although there are variations in the design of these two shedding mechanisms, there are only two basic principles of shed formation.

The counterbalanced loom is basically a four-shaft loom, although models with a greater number of shafts are used for damask weaving. Within the four-shaft limitation any weave can be constructed and the repeat length is unlimited.

The countermarch loom may have up to sixteen shafts, but the selection of shed formations is limited to the number of pedals – because each pedal is tied up to the shafts in a predetermined pattern that forms one sequence of warp-weft intersections when it is pressed down. Although

this has obvious limitations, it allows for the use of a greater number of shafts and gives a better shed formation. Whereas the pedal tie-up has to be pre-planned, the pedalling sequence does not, nor is there a limit on the repeat length.

Dobby looms may have up to twenty-four shafts. The shaft movement is controlled by an automatic mechanism of pegged lags or perforated cards (see page 35). The dobby's shedding mechanism imposes no restriction on the choice of weave construction, but the pegging of the lags has to be pre-planned so designing on the loom is very limited. The repeat length is also limited by the number of lags the dobby can carry or the number available.

Table looms vary greatly in construction, shedding action, and in the number of shafts, ranging from the portable rigid heddle to the complex sixteen-shaft loom. Because they are designed to be easily transported and stored, their length and width is kept to a practicable minimum. Their width is also limited by the fact that the shed has to be kept small to reduce the tension on the raised ends, and this slows down the passage of the shuttle. In a four-shaft loom the weaving width is limited to 90 cm (36 in) and in a sixteen-shaft loom to less than 60 cm (24 in).

The more sophisticated table looms are ideal for teaching, designing on the loom, or weaving small trial pieces, because only the drafts and the setting have to be pre-planned. No pedal tie-up is involved, nor is it necessary to have a prepared lifting plan – although when choosing a draft it is necessary to have some idea of what the final cloth will look like. A complex table loom will weave cloth of any weight or quality. Although the

General features of a loom
with a rising shed
(only one beam is in use):
A Warp beam
B Back bar
C Warp

D Loom frame
E Shafts
F Batten
G Reed
H Shuttle
I Breast bar

J Cloth
K Knee bar
L Cloth beam
M Lever to turn
cloth beam
N Pedals

Photo: Derrick Witty

weaving process itself tends to be slow and un-rhythmical, dressing the loom can be done quickly and easily.

GENERAL FEATURES OF LOOMS

Most table looms have a set of leavers to raise the shafts. The shedding mechanism of a floor loom can be operated by pedals – as on the counter-balanced and countermarch looms – or by a dobby. Each system is discussed in detail on pages 27 to 38. But whichever mechanism is used all looms have a number of features in common.

The warp beam

The function of the warp beam is to hold the warp ends, which are wound round it. It lies in supporting brackets at the back of the loom frame and is fitted with a cloth apron that reaches nearly to the shafts. The purpose of the apron is to allow the end of the warp to be brought close to the shafts.

The warp beam should be at least 12 cm (4¾ in) in diameter. The apron should be made of strong, firm cloth, cut several centimetres wider than the maximum width of the warp. One end is tacked to the beam, and an apron stick lies in a hem sewn along the other. Double cords pass through a line of holes in the cloth placed approximately 25 cm (10 in) apart immediately behind the stick (see page 146). The cords hold the portee stick at a distance of about 2·5 cm (1 in). Both sticks must be absolutely parallel to the beam or the warp circumference will be affected.

A very long warp has a tendency to slip sideways on the beam. This can be prevented by fitting movable flanges set at the required warp width. Such a beam does not have an apron, but has a rod that slots into the beam and cord extensions to hold the second rod to which the portee stick is tied.

The warp tension

The tension of the warp affects both the shed formation and the density of picking, and thus influences the texture and handle of a cloth. Changes in warp tension during weaving cause the pick density to vary, i.e. the greater the warp tension, the closer the picks will pack together.

One of two systems can be used to control warp tension in the floor looms:

FIXED TENSION CONTROL A ratchet wheel on one end of the beam engages with a pawl attached to the loom post, and this prevents the beam from unwinding toward the shafts. To turn the warp forward the pawl must first be lifted by hand or with a lever or cord from the front of the loom.

It is essential to keep the warp tension constant, and it should be carefully adjusted whenever a length of warp is wound forward. (This is parti-cularly necessary with an inelastic warp yarn.) The warp beam lies below the level of the shafts, so the warp is passed over a back rest (bar) above the beam to bring it up to the level of the heald eyes. This increases the length of warp between beam and shafts, and improves the yarn's elasticity.

Compound cloth constructions may need more than one warp and a second beam can be placed above the first. A second back bar is then necessary. To keep both warps at the right tension requires great care and it is advisable to wind the cloth forward frequently.

Separate selvage bobbins, tensioned by their own friction brake, cannot be used when the warp has a fixed tension control.

ELASTIC TENSION CONTROL This is a friction brake that does not have to be released when the cloth is wound forward and so keeps the warp under an even tension; at the same time it allows the beam to oscillate slightly when the pick is beaten down and the warp to unwind fractionally to compensate for yarn take-up in the cloth. The

Two warp beams placed one above the other, with corres-ponding back bars. Photo: Derrick Witty

friction brake is commonly used in dobby looms, but there is no reason why it should not be employed in a counterbalanced or countermarch loom.

There are various ways to apply a friction brake:
1 A weight box is the most convenient braking system for a hand loom. The length of the box depends on the length of the beam, and it should be about 20 cm (8 in) high and 15 cm (6 in) wide. Tie one strong smooth rope firmly at either end of the lower cross beam, then wind each two or three times (from front to back) around the warp beam at a point directly above. Attach one rope to a hook at each end of the weight box and suspend it as close to the floor as possible. Heavy objects are placed in the box to provide the weight.
2 For a more resilient tension, use a weight box or two separate weights and suspend lighter counterweights to the other end of the brake cords instead of attaching them to the tie beam.
3 A second braking method is to pivot a long lever on one side of the loom frame below the beam, with a cord, providing the brake, attached at one end. This is wound round the beam and

tied to the lower bar as before, and the brake is controlled by the position of a weight suspended at the other end of the lever. The system may appear unbalanced, but it keeps the tension even right across the warp.

Warp beams with an elastic tension control are sometimes placed at the same level as the shafts, so the warp ends do not run over a back bar. If a second beam is used, attach an additional set of supporting brackets to the inside of the loom posts, or extend the length of the loom.

A loom that has both a ratchet wheel and pawl, and a beam wide enough to accommodate an elastic tension system, is a most versatile tool. For rug and tapestry weaving fixed tension is essential, whereas elastic tension is better for weaving fabrics.

The cloth beam
At the front of the loom the woven cloth winds off on to a cloth beam or roller. In most hand looms this beam is placed inside the loom below the knee bar, and in this position holds a considerable amount of cloth. A ratchet and pawl prevent the

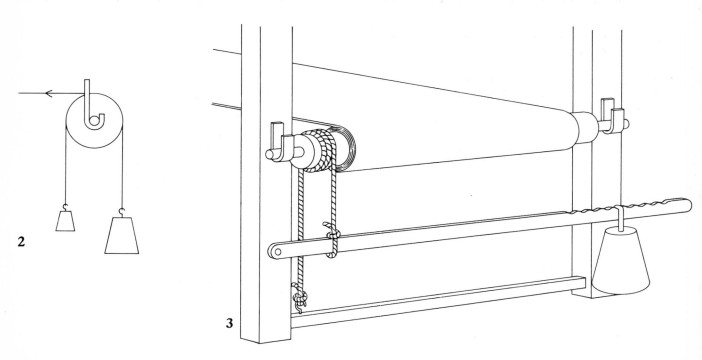

2

3

1 A weight box gives the most convenient friction brake for a hand loom. Photo: Derrick Witty

2 For a more resilient tension suspend a lighter counterweight to the other end of each brake cord.

3 A weighted lever provides an alternative method.

(*right*) Loom extended to carry two warp beams.

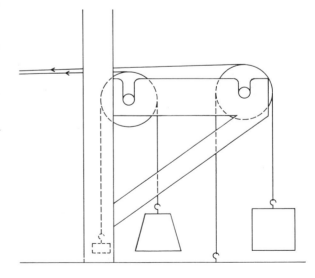

beam from turning back and unwinding the cloth, and an apron is attached. The apron extends over both the knee bar and the breast bar to within a short distance of the reed. A starting stick is attached to the apron stick which is slotted into the hem in the same way as the portee apron stick (see page 20). Both sticks must be perfectly parallel to the cloth beam.

Unfortunately most floor looms are constructed so that the cloth beam cannot be removed without taking the loom apart. But by cutting a piece the width of the beam axle out of each supporting post, the cloth beam can be slipped in and out fairly easily. And by fixing a metal plate on the outside of the cut-out pieces, they can be screwed back firmly in position.

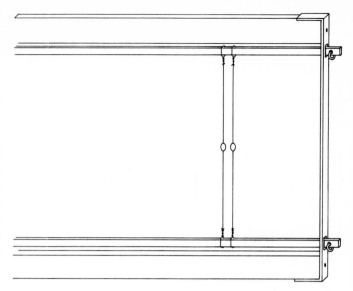

The heavy industrial-type frame shafts with wire or steel healds are essential for a dobby loom.

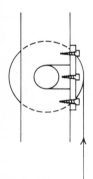

To make it possible to remove the cloth beam from a floor loom, small pieces can be cut out of the supporting posts and screwed back with metal plates.

The shafts

The shafts control the movement of the warp ends, i.e., they raise and/or lower them to form a shed opening for the passage of the weft. Shafts are frames, suspended in the loom, which carry string heddles or wire healds with a loop or eye in the centre through which the ends are threaded.

There are two main types of shaft. The lightweight shafts, which can be used in counterbalanced looms and are essential for countermarch looms, consist of a pair of sticks with varnished string heddles stretched between them (see illustration, page 32). Cords tied from end to end of each stick prevent the heddles from sliding off.

The industrial-type frame shaft essential for a dobby loom (see page 34) is heavy. The healds are

made of wire or steel and if the shafts are longer than about 60 cm (24 in) they will need a clip in the centre to prevent the heald-carrying rods from bending. These shafts can also be used in a counterbalanced loom.

A heddle should have an eye about 1 cm ($\frac{2}{5}$ in) long. This will be large enough for all but the coarsests yarns.

(*opposite*) Fancy yarns:
A Two-colour worsted slub, fibre dyed
B Woollen bouclé
C Acrylic slub, dope dyed
D Bulked synthetic yarn
E Brushed mohair, yarn dyed
F Brushed mohair yarn irregularly wrapped round cotton base
G Irregular worsted bouclé, yarn dyed
H Worsted loop, containing a percentage of dyed fibre
I Cotton gimp
J Rough-spun jute, natural colour
K Regular cotton slub
L Woollen spiral, yarn dyed

A

B

C

D

E

F

G

H

I

J

K

L

The batten

The batten is situated in front of the shafts and has three functions: to hold the reed (see page 31); to support the passage of the shuttle as it carries the weft pick through the shed; and to beat up the weft. The weaver pulls the batten forward to beat the pick up to the fell of the cloth.

THE OVERSLUNG BATTEN is suspended by swords from a rocker bar extending across the top of the loom, and is pivoted at either end. (It must swing freely to allow rhythmical weaving.) Because the shuttle race – a wooden bar at the front of the batten – has to support the shuttle on its passage through the shed and the warp level sometimes varies (see page 30), the batten's height is adjustable. The rocker bar can be raised or lowered by screws, or the position of the swords can be altered by pegs or by twisted cords.

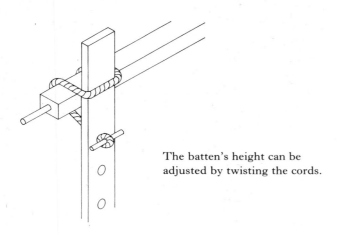

The batten's height can be adjusted by twisting the cords.

THE UNDERSLUNG BATTEN is pivoted at the base of the loom. It does not swing freely, but is often preferred because the shuttle race slopes toward the reed, making a better support for the shuttle.

(*opposite*) A curving twill is made by varying the density of both the ends and the picks. The cloth has a worsted warp and rough spun linen weft.

The fly-shuttle batten

The use of a fly-shuttle batten can increase weaving speed considerably by forcing the shuttle through the shed by the impact of a picker. The shuttle travels between two shuttle boxes, and the batten may have one or more sets fitted on each side. These are raised or lowered to present the shuttle carrying the right yarn colour to the picker. The fly-shuttle batten may be under- or overslung. The extensions required for the fly-shuttle batten increase the loom's width by at least 36 cm (14 in) on either side.

The reed

The reed is a coarse comb that holds the ends parallel between its metal divisions and helps to separate them as the shed changes. It is carried by the batten and after the pick has passed through the shed is pulled forward to beat the pick against the fell of the cloth.

The spaces between the metal divisions in the reed are known as 'dents', and the number of dents is termed the 'reed count' – which is measured in either decimetre or inch units (see page 64). The count and the length of the reed will be stamped on the binder rod at one end.

Apart from these purely practical functions, the reed can influence a cloth's design. For instance, during the weaving process it can be used to emphasize the characteristics of the weave construction: ends unevenly spaced in the reed will result in a vertically striped cloth, while by varying the strength of the reed impact the density of the picks is affected, creating horizontal bands.

When a heavy reed impact is required, the loom must be well enough constructed to withstand this without too much vibration. If the loom tends to slip forward attach foam-rubber pads to the base of the loom posts.

THE SHEDDING MECHANISMS

The shedding action of a loom separates the warp ends that are to lie above the pick from those that are to lie below it, making a space or 'shed' through which the weft is laid. This interlacing of the two sets of thread forms a web construction. The lifting or lowering of warp ends is controlled by the movement of the shafts.

A distinction is made between two types of shed formation: the centre shed and the rising shed. (There is a third type, the sinking shed, but it is rarely used.)

In a loom with a centre shed the shafts either rise or fall from the central position to make the shed. Thus, as no shaft is stationary when the shed is open, no end is either, and all the ends remain under equal tension and rise or fall only half the distance required for the full opening.

In a loom with a rising shed, the shed is formed by raising some shafts while the rest remain stationary. This imposes an extra tension on the raised ends. The degree of extra tension is directly related to the length of the loom, because this determines the angle at which the ends rise to form the shed.

THE COUNTERBALANCED LOOM

The counterbalanced loom is basically a four-shaft loom with a centre shed. The shafts are suspended at a distance of about one-fifth of the total width, at either side. Their balancing movement is controlled by a pair of pulleys from which pairs of pulleys or horses are suspended to provide the pivot centre for the shaft suspension. Poles,

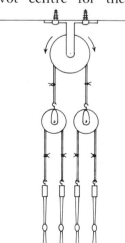

The balancing movement of the shafts is controlled by pulleys.

fitted with suspension chains and extending above the shafts, are an alternative form of shaft-movement control. Opinions differ as to the advantages and disadvantages of one system over the other.

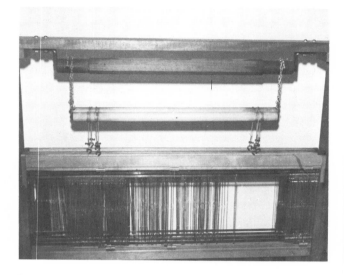

Poles fitted with suspension chains are an alternative system. Photo: Victor Edwards

When suspending the shafts, stretch a thread from the back bar to the breast bar of the loom and line up the heddle eyes level with the thread. Either industrial-type frame shafts or shafts carrying varnished string heddles can be used in a counterbalanced loom. Because the shafts are suspended from both ends, spare heddles or healds do not have to be distributed at either side of the shafts to balance the weight as in the dobby and table looms.

Four lams are pivoted at the side of the loom below the shafts and provide the central downward pull. Each shaft is tied to a lam. There are usually six pedals and these are attached to the lams in one of two ways:

1 One lam is attached to one pedal. The remaining two pedals are tied up for plain weave, i.e. one pedal to lams one and three, the other to lams two and four as these are so frequently used (see page

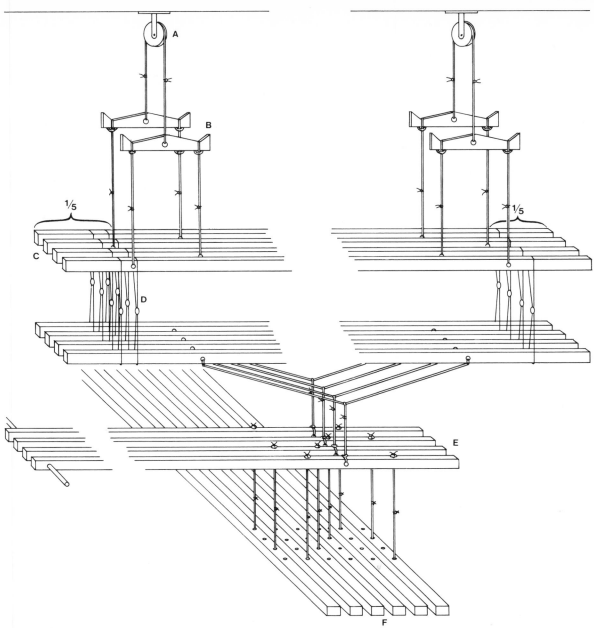

65). Thus to form a shed opening you may have to press down one pedal or two or three pedals at the same time depending on how many of the shafts need to be lowered to make the shed. Any shed formation is possible within the limitation of the four shafts, and there is no restriction on the length of the repeat.

The counterbalanced loom:

A Pulley	**D** Heddles
B Horses	**E** Lams
C Shafts	**F** Pedals

2 Alternatively, the pedals may be tied up in a predetermined pattern, i.e each pedal is tied to one, two or three lams and the shed is formed by pressing only one pedal. But even with six pedals, only six different shed formations are possible with this sort of tie-up, so variety is limited. On the other hand weaving is faster because only one pedal has to be pressed at a time. Pedalling can be in any sequence and there is no limit to the repeat length.

On a counterbalanced loom pulling down one pedal causes the rest to rise. In other words only the downward pull is a direct consequence of the pedal tie-up and pedal depression (see page 57). The shed is balanced when the same number of shafts is raised and lowered; and the ends go up and down at the same angle. But if only one shaft is lowered and the rest rise, the lowered ends tend to lie above the shuttle race (see page 27), giving less support to the shuttle passage. When three shafts are lowered and only one rises, the lowered ends lie lower and tend to be pushed up by the shuttle race, making the shed smaller. Neither situation is entirely satisfactory, but the problem can be overcome by using a batten with a spring-loaded shuttle race which responds to the shed position. (Unfortunately this precludes the use of a fly shuttle.)

The pedals can be pivoted at the back or the front of the loom according to personal preference. The shafts must be firmly tied together to neutralize the balancing system when the pedals are tied up or any adjustment has to be made to the cords. When they are pivoted at the back, tie them just high enough almost to touch the floor when depressed. All cords are joined by a snitch knot (see page 146), which allows for easy adjustment. Some looms are fitted with chains in place of cords.

THE COUNTERMARCH LOOM

Countermarch looms form a centre shed and their shafts are lifted by the counter movement of pivoted pairs of jacks and lams. Up to sixteen shafts can be used. Unlike the counterbalanced loom, each shaft makes a positive movement up or down, so the proportion of raised to lowered shafts does not affect the shed in any way. There are as many pedals as the loom has shafts. Each pedal is tied according to a pre-planned shed formation. Although only one pedal can be pressed down at a time, the pedalling sequence is entirely unrestricted. Any number of shafts can be used out of the full complement in a loom.

A shaft, a pair of jacks, and an upper (shorter) and lower (longer) lam form a unit in the shedding mechanism. The jacks are pivoted in a frame placed well above the shafts. The lams are pivoted at the side of the loom between shaft and pedals. The shaft in each unit is suspended from the outer ends of its pair of jacks, with the height of the heddle eyes just above the level of the breast and back bars.

The inner ends of the jacks should be about 4 cm ($1\frac{1}{2}$ in) apart. They are connected by a cord 25 cm (10 in) long, from which hangs a double cord that passes in front of the shaft and the upper lam of the unit, and is attached by a snitch knot to the cord of the lower lam. (This means that the cord actually passes through the centre of the warp.) The upper lam is tied by a snitch knot to a cord attached to the shaft. Thus, by pulling down a lower lam the inner ends of the jacks are pulled down, causing the outer ends to rise and to pull up the shaft. As the shaft rises it pulls up the upper lam belonging to the unit. Conversely, pulling down an upper lam will lower the shaft, pull the outer ends of the jacks down, and raise the inner ends and the lower lam of the unit. In other words, upper lams lower the shafts; lower lams raise them. Both movements draw some lams toward each other; to keep them out of each other's way tie the upper lams to tilt slightly upward, and the lower ones slightly downward. The combined

(*opposite*) Countermarch looms form a centre shed and may have up to sixteen shafts. Photo: Andrew Watson

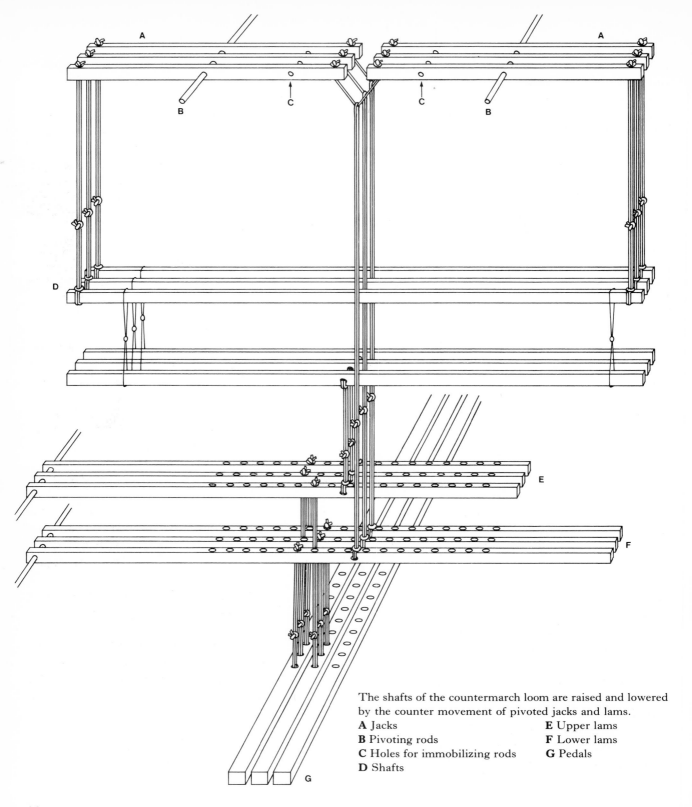

The shafts of the countermarch loom are raised and lowered by the counter movement of pivoted jacks and lams.

A Jacks
B Pivoting rods
C Holes for immobilizing rods
D Shafts
E Upper lams
F Lower lams
G Pedals

32

weight of both the shaft and upper lam of a unit should be as similar as possible to the weight of the lower lam by itself. So the shafts should consist of light wooden sticks and varnished string heddles. Industrial frame shafts can not be used as they are too heavy.

Tying up the pedals

Each pedal has a row of holes, each hole corresponding to holes in the lams above. The pedal holes are permanently fitted with cord loops. Prepare two bundles of double cords; a long set for the upper lams, and a shorter set for the lower.

Before tying the pedals or making any adjustment to the lam or pedal ties, immobilize the jacks by pushing the metal rods through the holes provided for this purpose in the jacks and loom frame. Support the pedals at the correct height for tying up. They should amost reach the floor when pressed down. Then sit in a convenient position inside the loom.

Place the cords in the lams according to the tie-up plan (see page 58), remembering that upper lams lower the shafts, lower lams raise the shafts, and that only one lam of each pair can be tied to the appropriate pedal. The pedals are tied up one by one, starting at the front of each, and each row of strings is placed in the lams ready to tie up the appropriate pedal below. Cords connecting the upper lam to the pedal *must* pass behind the lower lam of the pair. All cords are joined by snitch knots (see page 146).

To form a perfect shed opening in front of the reed, the shed should be slightly wider toward the back shafts. This is done by tying each pedal cord slightly tighter than the one before it. This tension differential along the pedal can be achieved in the following way: while pulling the cord tight in the loop of the snitch knot and tying it, press down the pedal with the left elbow (or right, if left-handed) just enough to allow it to rise a fraction with every tie added. Thus the last cords will be tight, while the front cords have a degree of slackness by the time all cords are tied.

An alternative method of achieving a tension differential in the lam-to-pedal tie-up is to raise the pivot point of the pedals while tying up to about 7cm ($2\frac{1}{2}$ in) above the normal level. In this case all cords must be tied with identical tension.

The shed formation is best in the countermarch loom when the number of shafts used and the number of pedals tied up are the same. When more shafts than pedals are required for a weave, the balance between shafts, lams, and pedals may need adjusting. For example, if the shafts tend to rise when the metal rods immobilizing the balance system are withdrawn, one or two pedals not used for the weave are tied on to the upper lams. If they tend to drop a little the pedals are tied to the lower lams. This balances the weight of the shafts.

A modified pedal tie-up

Many weavers find it uncomfortable to sit inside the loom to tie up the pedals, and consider this a disadvantage of using the countermarch loom. Mr Smith of Cambridge has devised an ingenious arrangement for extending the cords that connect the lams and pedals to the back of the loom, where they can be more easily handled.*

A strong board is attached to the back of the loom so that it slopes outward below the beam at an angle of about 20 degrees. As many pairs of holes as there are pedals are drilled in vertical rows down the board. Screw bolts with nuts and washers are placed beside each hole. A guide bar is placed across the width of the loom above the pedal pivot rod.

The pedals themselves do not have holes, but strong ring screws along the top. Cords are attached to the lams which are long enough to pass through a ring screw, along the pedal, under the guide bar, and out through a hole in the board. The cords from both the upper and lower lam of a unit are threaded through the appropriate ring

---

* Discussed in 'A simplified tie-up for double countermarch loom' by Peter Collingwood, *Quarterly Journal of the Guilds of Weavers, Spinners and Dyers* No. 49, March 1964.

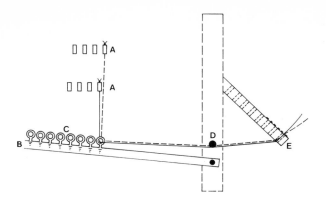

A modified countermarch-loom tie-up:
A Lams   **B** Pedal   **C** Ring screws
D Guide bar   **E** Board

screw and separated as they emerge from under the guide bar and passed one through each of a pair of holes in the board. All cords from the upper lams should go to one side, and all the lower ones to the other. One of the two cords is pulled tight and fastened with the nut, depending on which lam is needed by the tie-up plan.

The advantage of this system is that all the cords are available at any time, and so changes in pedal tie-up can be made very easily. The only disadvantage is that the cords wear out rather quickly where they pass through the ring screws and have to be replaced frequently.

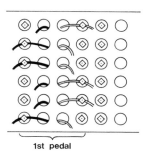

1st pedal

Two vertical rows of holes represent one pedal. Cords from upper lams are attached to one side, those from lower lams to the other.

The single jack-set countermarch loom

Some loom makers recommend, and many weavers prefer, a vertically placed jack mechanism for the countermarch loom, and it is essential for

wide looms. This mechanism has only one set of jacks, and the cords connecting them to the lower lams are outside the loom frame (see illustration). The cords suspending the shafts are passed over pulleys and attached to the shaft about one-fifth of their length from each end. The advantage of this arrangement is that the shafts are less likely to bend under the strain of the warp when the shed is open and no cords pass through the warp. The lam-to-pedal tie-up remains the same.

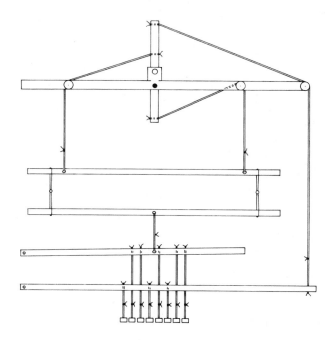

THE DOBBY LOOM

The shed is formed by rising shafts and most dobbies built for hand looms have sixteen, though a twenty-four-shaft dobby can be used if the loom is sufficiently long. The loom frame must be sturdy enough to carry the dobby's weight and also to withstand its vibration. A frame with a weaving width of more than 60 cm (24 in) will be at least 1·8 m (6 ft) high, so you will need 3 m (10 ft) between floor and ceiling to allow enough room for the action of the dobby mechanism.

The dobby mechanism
set up for weaving.
Photo: Philip Sayer

The principal features of a dobby mechanism are as follows:

1 The single pedal is pivoted at the back of the loom.

2 The shafts are suspended from a row of spring-controlled hooks.

3 A knife is fitted into a rising and falling frame.

4 A rotating cylinder carries a chain of lags that are pre-pegged according to a lifting plan (see illustration).

When the pedal is pressed down the knife rises, carrying with it all the hooks that lie in its passage, raising the shafts suspended from them. Release the pedal, and the knife, hooks and shafts fall back to their original position. The cylinder turns to the next lag and a new selection of hooks is placed over the knife for the next shed.

The shafts have to fall back under their own weight, with only a little assistance from the warp tension, so the heavy industrial frame shafts with metal healds must be used. If additional weight is needed, for instance if the warp ends tend to stick together, fix flat weights to the bottom of the shafts. This is preferable to the method of attaching a spring to either side of the shafts since these can seldom be tensioned equally. Distribute spare healds equally at either side of the shaft.

The dobby action is automatic. Each lag represents one shed, and as they have to rotate in sequence the shed order is predetermined. Slight design variations can be made by reversing the direction of the cylinder rotation, or by not inserting a pick into every shed opening. But for major alterations the lags have to be re-pegged.

Some dobbies have a reversed lifting action: the hooks stand over the knife and are pressed *out* of its way by the pegs. The lags should be pegged in reverse order, otherwise the cloth will be woven face down. If the cloth construction requires most of the ends to be lifted most of the time, it will take considerable effort to press down the pedal. Providing the dobby works well and you are a careful weaver, it is easier to weave such cloths face down.

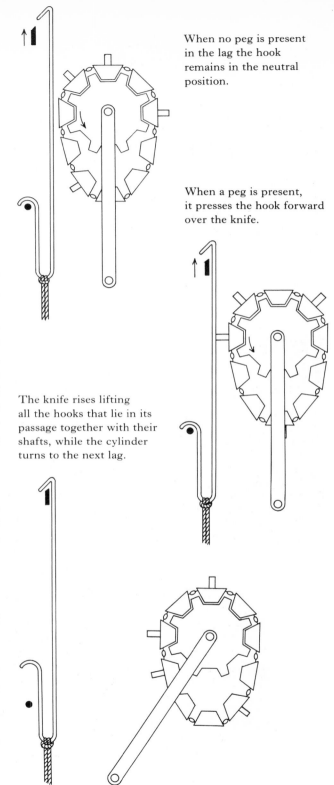

When no peg is present in the lag the hook remains in the neutral position.

When a peg is present, it presses the hook forward over the knife.

The knife rises lifting all the hooks that lie in its passage together with their shafts, while the cylinder turns to the next lag.

Pegging the lags: each row or lag represents one shed.
Photo: Philip Sayer

An eight-shaft table loom. Photo: Andrew Watson

TABLE LOOMS

Table looms are available with up to sixteen shafts. Most table looms with more than four shafts have a set of levers on each side to raise the shafts. If the shafts are suspended centrally, spare heals must be distributed in equal groups on either side of the warp, in order to keep the balance even. The warp tension is controlled by ratchet wheel and pawl. Some looms have two beams so it is possible to weave cloths that require more than one warp.

All table looms have a rising shed and, because of their comparative shortness, lift the ends at a very steep angle. This puts them under considerable tension, and makes a good shed formation difficult, particularly with an inelastic yarn when the warp tension has to be fairly loose to form a

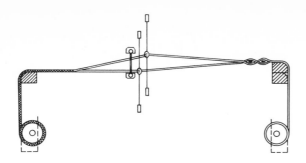

The back of the table loom can be raised with a piece of wood to reduce the tension on the raised ends.

shed at all. In this situation weaving is difficult, because the raised ends are very tight, while those not lifted are too slack. The remedy is to raise the level of the warp at the back of the loom by tying, or clamping, a length of wood about 4 to 5 cm (1½ in) high on top of the back bar, thus reducing the angle of the shed behind the shafts. It is also helpful to take the shed sticks out of the warp while weaving, unless they are absolutely vital to separate the ends.

The tension of the raised ends also affects the position of the lower warp ends, which should be supported by the shuttle race in front of the batten. If the raised ends are tight they tend to pull up the cloth at the front of the loom, and raise the lower ends above the shuttle race, which means the shuttle has to run through the shed without any firm support beneath it. This problem becomes more acute the more shafts there are, and warps wider than about 60 cm (24 in) are then very difficult to cope with.

DESIGNING FOR THE POWER LOOM

The differences between the hand and the power looms are not as great as is often imagined, and the restraints that the industrial designer has to accept may well be economic rather than mechanical. The basic principles of weaving are the same for both loom types, but the power loom's speed makes no concessions to yarns that are tender, weak, or have a low abrasion resistance – which does limit the choice of the warp yarns.

It is quite possible, in fact, and more economic, to weave initial cloth samples and prototypes by hand; provided the designer is familiar with both the scope and limitations of the particular power loom to be used for bulk production, and takes these into account from the beginning.

A valuable criterion to remember when designing for the power loom is that you cannot possibly produce a good fabric on a power loom if it has caused weaving difficulties on the hand loom.

When designing for power-loom production the following factors must be considered:

1 The warping method, affecting the maximum number of warp yarn packages that can be assembled in one section.

2 Whether the loom can accommodate one or more beams. When weaving long lengths of cloth differential yarn take-up is very important. Although a short length of fabric that shows only a slight slacking of some ends can be woven in a hand loom on one beam, it would require two beams for bulk production.

3 The maximum number of shafts the loom can take. (Here the designer may find that the power loom has more than the hand loom used for samples.)

4 Its shedding mechanism and repeat limitations.

5 The method of pick insertion. (Most of the recent developments in power-loom design affect the pick insertion. And though some of the new methods have increased the loom's scope, others impose limitations.)

6 How many weft yarns/colours can be used in one design. Whether the yarn/colour change can be done at either side of the warp. Whether there is a limit to the number of different yarn counts that can be used in one design.

7 Whether there are limitations within the range of yarn sizes.

8 The cloth 'take-up' mechanism. (The number of picks in a measured unit is regulated by the rate at which the cloth moves forward, so it is not possible on all power looms to vary pick density within a repeat unit.)

3 Preparing to weave and weaving methods

Preparing the warp and dressing the loom take as much, if not more, time than the weaving itself. It is essential that all these processes are carried out with care, since only then can a perfect cloth be produced. Once the warp is in the loom and the ends threaded through the shafts and reed, it becomes very time consuming and sometimes extremely difficult to alter the warp setting or colour arrangement or to change the draft. While the weft packages (bobbins or pirns) must be wound with care so that the yarn unwinds evenly, the weft can be changed freely and so can the density of picking. The ease with which the weave construction can be changed depends on the shedding mechanism of the loom. In any case the weave construction is related to the draft (see page 55), to change which requires rethreading the warp in the shafts.

PREPARING THE WARP

The warp threads – or ends as they are called – run parallel through the length of a cloth. During the weaving process these threads are held by the warp beam at the back and the cloth beam at the front end of the loom and are stretched through it under tension. The reed's dents distribute the ends evenly across the width of the cloth, and their upward and downward movement is controlled by shafts, through which they must be threaded in the pre-planned sequence.

The warp is made on a warping mill or board, which is used to measure out the ends to the correct length – so that they are equally tensioned when wound on to the warp beam – and to arrange them in the right order.

The ends are wound on to the mill or board in groups often called 'portees'. The number of ends in a portee depends on the number of packages of yarn available, the size of the yarn creel that holds them, or the number of ends in the repeat if the warp is striped. A portee should not be too bulky, so group fewer ends together if the yarn is coarse.

Before you can start warping, the total number of ends in the warp must be calculated, and the number of portees established (see page 14). When a warp is made up of more than one type of yarn and/or colour, the sequence of their placing within the repeat has to be stated in a warping plan (see page 144).

Warping equipment

YARN PACKAGES AND THE YARN CREEL To make an even warp it is essential to run the yarn evenly on to the warping mill. If taken straight from the hank it is difficult to retain a regular tension, so yarn packages such as a spool, cone or cop are used for this process. Spools, reels or bobbins rotate on the spindles of a yarn creel, and the yarn is drawn forward towards the warping mill. Cones stand on their own base, the yarn being pulled off upward through a guide hook; cops require a supporting peg. If the yarn slides down over the cone, place its base in a rubber ring that is wider than the full cone to prevent the yarn from catching underneath.

A large yarn creel that will hold up to forty or more yarn packages is a great advantage, particularly if it is designed to hold all types of package – as it it quite possible to use a variety when warping on the vertical warping mill or warping board.

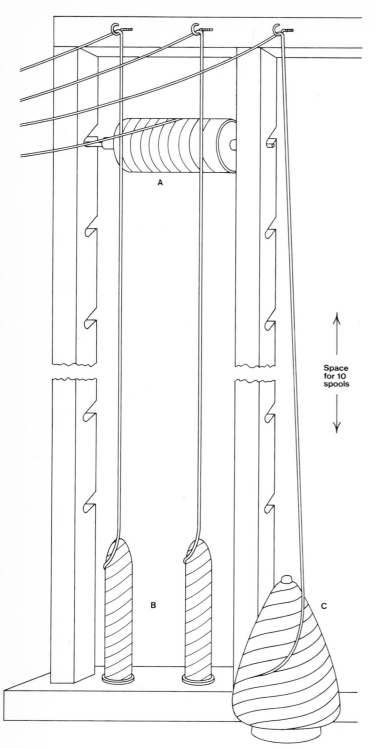

THE LEASE REED The yarn from the packages in the yarn creel are threaded through the lease reed before the warp can be made on the mill or board. This is a coarse reed with alternate closed and open dents used to make the 'lease cross' – the crossing of the ends in the warp that keeps the ends in the right sequence. It is mounted on a firmly based stand at about shoulder height. A density of 24 per dm (6 per in) is recommended.

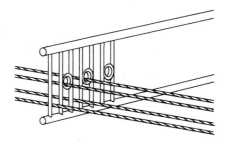

The lease reed.

(*left*) A large yarn creel that will hold up to forty yarn packages is a great advantage.
A Spool (reel or bobbin)
B Cops
C Cone

Space for 10 spools

THE VERTICAL WARPING MILL The vertical warping mill resembles a very large upright reel, which rotates on a central axle (see illustration right). Either four or six frames extend outward from the axle, and the circumference of the mill may be anything between 2 and 10 metres (7–33 ft). Two cross bars, each carrying two upright pegs, are set at eye level between adjacent frames. The two pegs on the left-hand bar are alternative starting pegs, and must be removable; the pair on the right-hand bar are the lease pegs for the lease cross. The first starting peg is used for warps that are made for floor looms, where the lease cross is required at a greater distance from the shaft; the second peg is used for warps destined for small counterbalance and table looms. The advantage of upright pegs is that the ends cannot accidentally slip off. A detachable cross bar, situated at a lower level than the starting and lease cross pegs, holds the two end pegs. These are mounted in a horizontal position. This cross bar can be clamped at any height, and between any two frames.

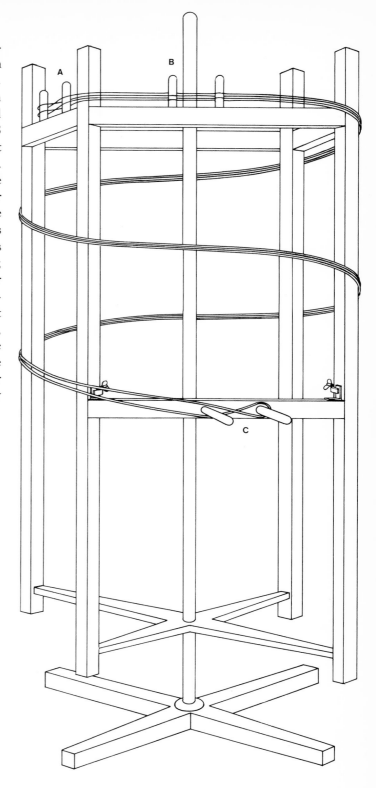

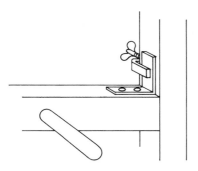

(*right*) The vertical warping mill:
A Starting pegs
B Lease cross pegs
C End pegs

THE HORIZONTAL WARPING MILL This mill is similar to the vertical mill, but may be turned by hand or electric motor. Its circumference can be as little as 2 metres (7 ft), but its length, which must be based on the greatest warp width a weaver will require, takes up considerable floor space. The warping is done in sections of warp, lying side by side over the width required.

The advantage of the horizontal warping mill is that the warp can be transferred directly on to the warp beam without chaining, which ensures an even tension on all the ends and cuts out the much more laborious method of spreading the portees and winding the warp on the beam by hand.

THE WARPING BOARD The warping board can be hung on the wall, and so has the advantage of taking up little space. The starting and lease cross pegs are placed at the top of the board, and a row of pegs runs down each side with two extra pegs at the bottom for the portee cross. The pegs are all placed horizontally to the hanging board, the two starting pegs must be removable, but the rest must be fixed firmly so that they do not slant toward each other under the tension of the portees. Warping on a large board is as efficient as on a vertical mill, and the warping method is the same. Alternatively the outer side of one of the loom frames can serve as a warping board if the loom is constructed on the 'four-poster' pattern. In this case the pegs must fit into holes deep enough to hold them firmly, yet can be taken out when not required.

Making a warp on the vertical warping mill

Establish the length of the warp on the mill by attaching a thread of the required warp length to the starting peg and winding it round in a downward spiral. Fix the cross bar holding the end pegs at the point where it finishes. Whether the first or second starting peg is used depends on the type of loom for which the warp is being made. For example, the table-loom warp should start from the second peg, because the lease cross (made on the lease pegs) must be near the beginning of the warp.

Place the yarn packages in the creel – in the order stated in your warping plan if using more than one yarn type or colour (see page 144). Put the lease reed in front of the creel and thread each end through a dent. The first end – which will be the first end in the warping plan – should be entered in a closed dent, the second in an open dent, and so on (see illustration on page 40). When all the ends in the portee (usually an even number) are threaded through the reed, tie them together and loop them over the appropriate starting peg.

Put the lease reed between the yarn creel and the warping mill (about 80 cm, or 32 in, from the mill) and stand by it with the creel on the right and the mill to your left. You are now ready to start warping.

With your right hand take hold of all the ends on the 'creel side' of the lease reed and pull the portee taut. As you lift your hand the even ends entered in the open dents will rise. On the 'mill side' of the reed put the first finger of your left hand through the gap between the raised and stationary ends. Now lower your right hand to bring the ends in the open dents below the stationary ones, and put the thumb of your left hand in this second opening. The ends should now cross each other between your finger and thumb. This is the lease cross.

Transfer the cross to the lease cross pegs (on the right-hand bar) by bringing your left hand forward to the mill, while your right still holds the portee taut. With the palm of your hand facing the mill, point your thumb and first finger downward and slip the threads off on to the pegs. The first thread of the portee is now the first thread on the warping mill.

Set the warping mill in motion (from right to left) with your left hand while you guide the portee with your right, and spiral the threads down to the end pegs. At this point make a 'portee cross' – to keep the portees in the right

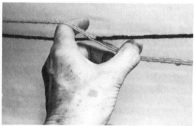

(*above and left*) Making the lease cross. Stand by the lease reed with the creel to the right and the mill on the left. Make the cross with the thumb and first finger of the left hand while holding the portee taut with the right. Photos: Derrick Witty (*left*) and Andrew Watson

(*below left*) Transferring the cross to the lease cross pegs: the palm of the hand faces the mill on the 'downward' rotation (seen here through the mill), and away from the mill on the 'upward'. Photos: Andrew Watson

order – by twisting them in a figure eight over the first peg, round the second end peg, and back under the first.

Reverse the rotation of the mill and spiral the portee back upward. When it reaches to 50 to 60 cm (about 2 ft) of the lease pegs, make another lease cross in exactly the same way as before. The first end in the portee must again be the first on the peg. To do this bring the left hand forward with the palm facing downward and the three free fingers lightly holding the portee in the hand. Point the first finger down to let the ends slip over the peg on the right, then move the hand slightly to the left to do the same with the thumb. Wind the portee round the starting peg and the cycle is complete. You now have two portees on the mill.

Repeat the process until you have turned the

required number of portees on to the mill. To prevent the portees building up on top of each other, wind each pair fractionally below the previous pair. Groups of portees must not overlap on the end pegs, so warps wider than 60 cm (24 in) or warps of coarse yarn must be made in two halves. If the warp is very densely set, it may be necessary to make it in four parts. In this case the sequence of the warps should be marked by some distinguishing tie at the first portee to avoid placing them on the beam in the wrong order.

When a warp is to be made with a complex stripe, use a large yarn creel and a longer lease reed, and place several portees at a time in the reed with a few empty dents between them. These portees can then be used in varying sequences and combinations.

It is possible to warp with an uneven number of ends and still to retain the regular sequence of the cross if on the upward run of the portee you form the lease cross in the reverse order. That is, if you first lower the right hand, place the first finger of the left in the opening, and then raise the portee for the thumb insertion.

If there is no lease reed available, the cross can be picked up with the fingers. Hold the portee taut with the left hand and pick up the cross with the thumb and first finger of the right. Starting with the last end in the creel place the first finger over the end and move it downward. Place the thumb over the next end and turn it downward. Bring the first finger up again over the next and move it downward, and so on. Transfer the cross to the lease pegs with the right hand.

Taking the warp off the warping mill

Both the lease cross and the portee cross have to be retained while the warp is transferred to the beam, so they must be secured with ties while still on the mill. Thread a cord long enough to be spread out over the whole width of the warp through each cross, and tie each to make a loose loop. Tie the bundle of portees firmly together about 1 metre (just over 1 yd) from the portee

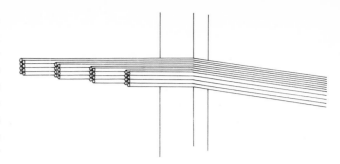

Wind each pair of portees on to the mill fractionally below the previous pair.

If there is no lease reed the cross can be picked up with the thumb and first finger of the right hand, while the left hand holds the portee taut.

cross, and make a loose tie through the starting loop of the warp. No other ties are required.

Remove the starting peg and flick the warp off the lease pegs. Make a loop at the starting end and, using your left hand as a crochet hook and your right to control the tension, loop the warp into a chain. Do not draw the end of the warp through the last loop or it will be difficult to start unchaining. Tie it up to prevent it slipping through accidentally. If the warp is very fine do not make a chain but wind it on to a smooth tube of metal or cardboard.

DRESSING THE LOOM
Four distinct processes are involved in dressing a loom: (1) beaming the warp, (2) threading the shafts, (3) threading the reed, and (4) tying up the warp. (Draft and reeding plans are discussed on pages 55 and 64.)

Equipment
THE RADDLE This is essentially a coarse reed, with round pegs and a removable cap, used to distribute the portees evenly across the warp beam. It is important for the cap to fit well over the teeth or the portees will slip from one dent to another when the warp is shaken. The cap can be secured at each end by a peg or with bolts and wing nuts.

CARDBOARD OR WARP STICKS Pieces of good quality cardboard are inserted between layers while beaming to give the warp firmness. Warp sticks are an adequate substitute, but paper is useless.

CROSS STICKS A pair of cross sticks is used to preserve the cross made during warping. They are essential to retain the correct sequence of the ends in the warp. Cross sticks for warps of wool, worsted, or fibrous yarns should be flat, so that they can be turned on edge when the threads need separating by hand before the sticks can be pushed back towards the back bar. Round cross sticks are better for fine, smooth yarn.

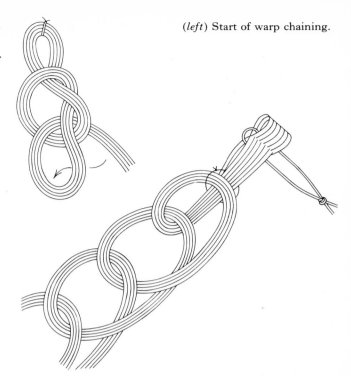

(*left*) Start of warp chaining.

Tie up the end of the warp chain to prevent it slipping through.

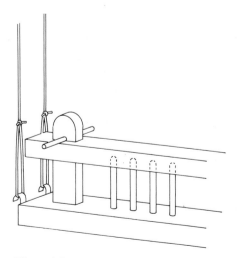

The raddle.

THREADING HOOK This is used for threading the shafts. A hook with a short, blunt end is used to thread all but the very coarsest yarns.

REED HOOKS The best reed hooks are made from hard wood or brass. They are more comfortable to hold if thicker at the holding end.

PORTEE AND STARTING STICKS These are used to attach the warp to the warp and cloth beam aprons respectively (see pages 20 and 24).

Beaming the warp

The warp, or warps, have to be wound on to the beam under maximum tension, and with the portees evenly distributed across the warp width by the raddle. It is an advantage to beam the warp a little wider than its weaving width to increase the tension on the outer ends.

Suspend the raddle from the loom frame at the back of the loom, so that it hangs level with either the back rest or the beam, depending on the type of loom. If the raddle is hung from a pair of hooks at each end of its base, the raddle cap can be removed without disturbing the suspension. The raddle must swing freely to minimize the danger of broken ends during beaming.

When dressing a table loom, stand or clamp the raddle on the table behind the loom, and stretch the warp out backward while beaming on.

To make room for the warp, divide the heddles in industrial frame shafts and push them to either side. The lightweight shafts used in a counter-march loom can be raised and held suspended with a pair of cords, or placed above the jacks, to get them out of the way.

Undo enough length of the warp chain (see page 45) and lay it through the loom so that the portee cross is at the warp-beam end. Place the portee stick through the end loop of the warp and secure it to the apron stick with the two outermost cords only (see opposite).

In order to keep both hands free while distributing the bundle of portees in the raddle, sup-

A grooved bobbin.

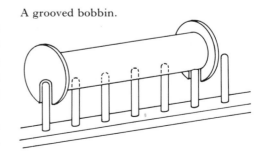

port them on a grooved bobbin or a bent piece of cardboard placed over the raddle's teeth.

Distribute each portee in a dent. If there are more portees than dents for the required warp width, some will have to be doubled up. If fewer portees, make sure that the empty dents are evenly spaced between them. *Never* split a portee. When all the portees are in the raddle fix the cap down over the teeth.

Pull the warp forward through the loom and out as far as possible in front; the farther the better. Hold the warp with a firm grip – if made in two sections take one in each hand – and shake it up and down, while pulling toward you at the same time. This evens out the portees on the portee stick. When they look straight and well distributed, you can tie the remaining apron cords and cut the firm tie made round the warp after warping (see page 44). The warp will fan out and, if well made, should be quite even in tension.

Hold the warp as taut as possible at the front of the loom while an assistant turns the beam. Walk forward with the warp as it is wound on, never let it slip through the hands. Each time more warp is released from the chain, shake it well before winding proceeds.

Never stroke or comb the warp with your fingers, it only makes uneven yarn tension worse. Unless it has been very badly made loose ends usually tighten up again as the warp is wound on.

Swing the raddle gently backward and forward while winding if the portees tend to stick together and get caught in its teeth. And if a broken end cannot with certainty be placed in its correct portee, run it over the raddle cap and return it to its proper position when the lease cross is reached.

When the warp on the beam begins to feel soft, give it a new firm base by winding a piece of cardboard or four or five warp sticks into one layer. If you put in a second or third set, place these directly above one another to give maximum support. Lay strips of thin paper between warp layers if the ends tend to slip off sideways. And it is advisable to reduce the warp's width gradually

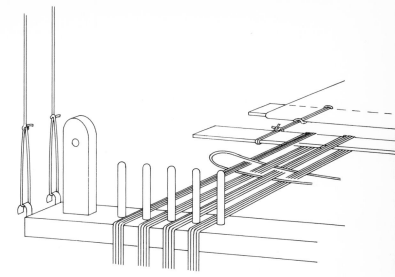

Place the portee stick through the end loop of the warp and secure it to the apron stick with the outermost cords only. Distribute the portees in the raddle. Never split a portee.

When the warp on the beam begins to feel soft, wind in four or five warp sticks (or a piece of cardboard) to give it a new firm base.

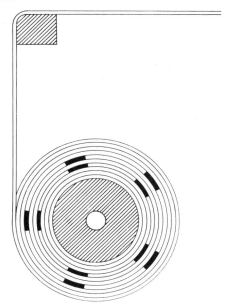

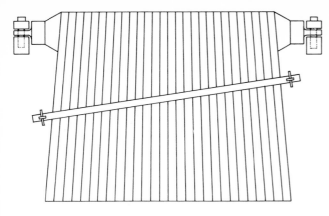

The warp width can be reduced by holding the raddle at a slight angle.

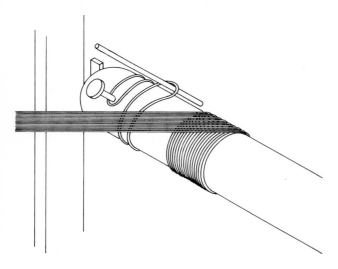

Temporary beam-turning device.

by holding the raddle at a slight angle to the beam.

When the lease cross is about 12 cm (5 in) behind the shafts, enough warp has been wound on. Fix the beam with ratchet and pawl or friction brake to prevent it unrolling (see page 20).

Replace the lease cord with a pair of cross sticks hung from the loom frame, and tie a cord from end to end below the warp to prevent them slipping out accidentally. In table looms the cross sticks are held by a pair of cords extending from back to front on either side of the warp.

If the warp beam does not have a handle the following efficient temporary device can easily be made. Drill a 4-cm (1½-in) hole into one end of the beam – beyond the warp width – and stand a metal peg in it. Take a circle of cord, loop one end over the peg and wind it backward round the beam. Put a winch handle in the other end. While stretching out a further length of warp, the winch handle can be braced against the loom frame.

Threading the shafts

To control the movement of the warp threads they must each be threaded through an eye of a heddle or heald. The threading is done according to the draft, a preplanned threading sequence (see page 55). This can be done more quickly if a 'reacher in', sitting beside the loom between the cross sticks and shafts, picks up the ends in the right order and reaches them to the threading hook. If you do not have any help, bring the cross as close to the shafts as possible and, keeping the section of the warp you are working from under tension (by tying it with a snitch knot to the front part of the loom), pick the ends from the cross one by one – working from left to right, right to left, or from the centre.

When two or more beams make up the warp (see page 21), each warp has its own cross sticks, and the lowest set should be suspended nearest the shafts. With a complex warp arrangement, the number of sticks required can become unwieldy, and it is better to retain the lease cords. Attach them one behind the other to a pair of cords stretched horizontally through the loom.

Threading mistakes can be avoided if the position of the ends in the cross is checked in relation to the threading repeat, i.e. if the threading repeat is on even ends, the last end of the repeat of the draft should always be in the same cross position. If it is on odd ends its position alternates in the cross.

Threading the reed

Lay the reed flat just below the heddle eyes between cords suspended from the loom frame. Pull the threads downward through the dents, and tie them loosely in groups to prevent them slipping back. When all the ends are through fix the reed in the batten and pull the ends forward. If the number of ends per dent is not regular throughout, a reeding plan should be prepared in advance (see page 64).

In the table loom the reed can be laid between the horizontal cords which also hold the cross sticks.

Tying up the warp

Tie up the ends in small groups, and while equalizing the tension, keep an eye on the cross behind the shafts, because it is here that the threads tend to stick together.

Start at one side and tie small groups of ends to the starting stick with the first part of a reef knot. Then, working from the centre alternately toward each side, tighten the knots by pulling both ends of the knot toward the reed (not upward) and complete the tie. This method will make the outer ends of the warp slightly tighter.

With a smooth warp yarn reef knots may not hold, in which case tie each group of ends together, attach a long knotless cord to one end of the starting stick and thread it between the ends and round the stick as in the illustration. Pull the cord tight each time it is passed under the stick. Make sure that the tension is evenly distributed across the warp width.

For pedal tie-ups see pages 56 to 60.

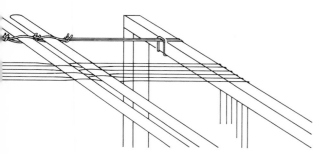

In table looms the cross sticks are held by a pair of cords on either side of the warp. In all other looms they are suspended from the loom frame.

Thread a cord through the knotted ends and round the starting stick if the warp yarn is too smooth for knots to hold over the stick.

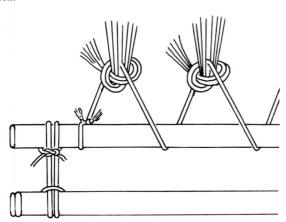

PREPARING THE WEFT YARN

The weft is wound on to a bobbin or pirn and is carried through the shed by a shuttle.

SHUTTLES A boat shuttle with rollers is suitable for all but the finest or coarsest yarns, and can be used with every type of loom with an ordinary batten. The yarn bobbin lies in a hole in the centre of the shuttle, and rotates on a spindle. The shuttle should be open at the top and bottom so that the fingers can easily control the bobbin's rotation. As the yarn is dispensed by the rotation of the bobbin, no twist is added to it; this type of shuttle is used when weaving with flat strips such as ribbons, leather thonging, etc. A shuttle with two bobbin spaces makes it possible to lay two threads at once, even if the bobbins unwind at different rates. There are smaller, heavier shuttles, without rollers, for use with fine yarns such as silk or rayon.

Boat shuttle.

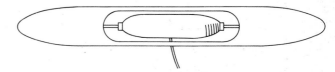

Two-bobbin shuttle.

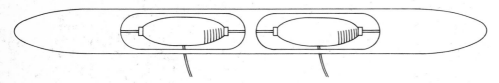

The pirn shuttle used in the fly-shuttle batten (see page 27) is heavier, and its metal tips make it unsuitable for hand throwing. The yarn's tension is controlled by the course it takes through the shuttle eye: it is drawn over the tip of the pirn and given one twist for each circumference wound off.

Pirn shuttle.

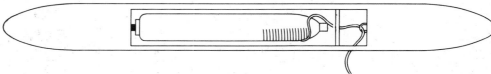

WINDERS The weft is wound on to a bobbin with a winder, which may be turned mechanically or by hand (or foot), but the yarn tensioning and shaping is always done by hand. A pirn winder can be fully mechanized. Take care not to overwind; a

(*opposite*) A lightweight woollen cloth with a freely formed weft distortion pattern. To make the distortions bundles of yarn are introduced between the picks during weaving, and removed after the finishing process.

50

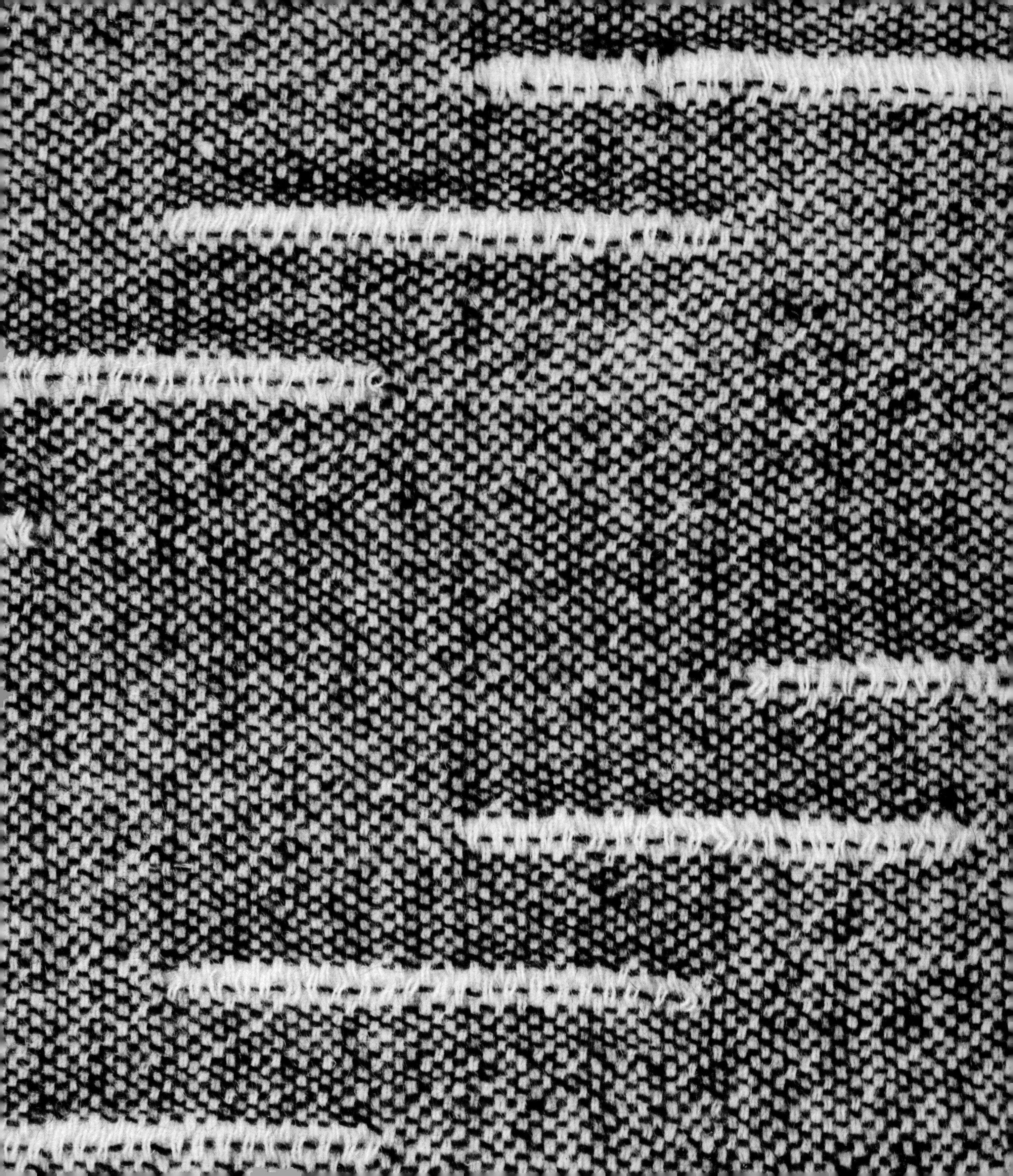

bobbin or pirn must never be so large that it touches the shuttle walls nor should a bobbin be too heavy or it will not rotate properly, so wind on less yarn if the weft is very fine. If the yarn tends to slide off line the shuttle wall with fur or fur-fabric.

WEAVING METHODS

The weaving process may appear to be a mechanical sequence of actions – pedal depression, shed opening, weft insertion and beating up. But to weave a great variety of cloth weights and qualities takes both skill and experience. A steady rhythm is essential for even weaving and a good weaver will only stop to replace a weft package or to tie a broken end.

The shed formation

To form a shed, press down the pedal of a floor loom or the appropriate levers of a table loom.

To achieve a clear shed formation with a dobby loom, press the pedal down firmly and quickly. With a countermarch, press the pedals more slowly. But if you have difficulty in getting a clear shed make a quick partial up-and-down movement first before depressing fully.

The pedalling sequence can affect the speed of weaving considerably. When yards of the same cloth are to be woven, it is important to plan the sequence of the pedals in an order that makes it possible to engage the feet alternately, and to make the pedal selection as easy as possible.

The shed opening

The timing of the shed opening and closing in relation to the batten movement has considerable influence on the picking density and quality of the

(*opposite*) The pattern of this plain-weave cloth is formed by linked and diverted ends. Six shafts are required, two for the ground weave and four for the linked ends. The yarn is an irregularly spun Fibro (rayon fibre) and linen mixture.

cloth. The usual rhythm is to open the shed by pressing down the pedal while at the same time pushing the batten back. By the time the shed is open the batten is in a position suitable for throwing the shuttle. Throw the shuttle through the shed and close it by releasing the pedal while swinging the batten forward. For a densely picked fabric, delay closing the shed until the pick is beaten up against the fell of the cloth. Keep the reed pressed momentarily against the pick and change the shed. Then, with the shed open and the pick locked between the raised and lowered ends, swing the batten back. This method of passing the reed through an open shed is also better for a closely set warp, or if the yarn has a low abrasion resistance because there is much less reed friction when the ends are not bunched together in the dents. Double beating in of the weft should be avoided, except for rug weaving.

Weaving with the boat shuttle

Weaving with a boat shuttle takes practice, the aim being to keep the weft tension even and to make a neat selvage. Although most weavers have their own views on how the shuttle should be thrown – and this also depends to some extent on the type of batten suspension and shed formation – it is important to pull the weft against the fell of the cloth at the selvage after each throw. When catching the shuttle as it emerges from the shed, stop the bobbin rotating with the fingers – through the opening in the base. Pull the shuttle out of the shed toward you so that you catch the pick between the selvage ends without pulling it and destroying the curve it has formed in the shed. This weft curve is important, because it provides sufficient extra yarn for the pick to be beaten tightly against the fell of the cloth. The slacker the picks the closer they will pack together in the cloth. As the height of the pick curve is the same whatever the cloth's width, a wider piece will inevitably have tighter picks which cannot be beaten so close together. It is important to remember this fact when weaving a narrow trial piece of a densely picked fabric

53

Weaving with the boat shuttle. Make an arc with the weft to provide enough extra yarn for the pick to curve under and over the ends.

so that the full width cloth can be woven with the identical pick density.

When using more than one shuttle, keep the shuttles you are not using parallel to the fell of the cloth and close to the selvage. Place the shuttles in an order that gives the best selvage.

Weaving with the pirn shuttle
This shuttle is used only in fly-shuttle battens. Keep one hand permanently on the centre of the batten cap, while the other controls the picker.

Swinging the batten
The batten is normally swung forward with one arm, though both can be used if you need a very heavy beat. Looms for fine cloths with little variation in the pick density usually have the batten placed slightly farther forward – it is pushed back while the shuttle is thrown and then swings forward under its own weight.

Broken ends
When ends break during weaving you can often discover the reason by observing at what point this happens. For instance, broken ends near the fell of the cloth usually indicate that the warp tension is too tight, particularly if the yarn has a low abrasion resistance. To help prevent it, relax the warp tension slightly and swing the reed through an open shed. Breaks near the reed, on the other hand, are often caused by a poor shed opening not giving the shuttle a clear run through the shed. And broken ends in the shafts are probably due to damaged or rough heddles, or because the cross sticks have been allowed to move too close to the shafts causing an acutely angled shed opening.

It is usually best to disconnect the cross stick suspension once weaving has started. There is then no danger of the cords being too short and pulling up the sticks. They move back more easily if they are not attached to each other.

4 Diagrammatic weave construction

The cloth construction (the intersecting of ends and picks), the sequence of the threading of the ends in the shafts, and the order of shaft movement have to be interpreted in diagrammatic form. A generally accepted shorthand system drawn on point paper, divided by bar lines into units of eight by eight squares to facilitate reading, has been evolved for the purpose of illustrating the weave construction, draft, and lifting instructions. (There are minor variations within the system, but they do not affect the principle of the notation.) The notation is essential for keeping worksheets and records (see page 144). Only by understanding the system can a designer/weaver have any real creative freedom.

Weave notation provides an accurate graphic representation of all end and pick intersections in the weave. How the ends and picks intersect each other is determined by the order in which the ends are entered in the shafts. This information is recorded in the *draft*. The order in which the shafts are raised to form the correct sheds for the design is represented either by a diagram of the *pedal tie-up* and *pedalling order* or by a *lifting plan*, depending on the type of loom. The *reed notation* shows exactly how the ends are to be entered in the reed and is important for both making the warp (see page 39) and dressing the loom (see page 45).

WEAVE NOTATION

The weave notation is a diagrammatic illustration of the cloth construction within the repeat unit. It is read from left to right and from bottom to top. Each vertical row of squares in the diagram represents one end (A in the illustration). Each horizontal row of squares represents one pick (B). Each square is therefore the crossing point of one end and one pick (C). An end lifted over a pick is represented by a solid square (D); a pick passing over an end is a blank one (E). Thus although a simple interpretation of the woven cloth could be drawn like this (F), the diagram (G) gives just as accurate a picture of the thread intersections and contains all the information needed to reproduce them.

DRAFT NOTATION

Draft notation illustrates the order in which the ends are threaded in the shafts.

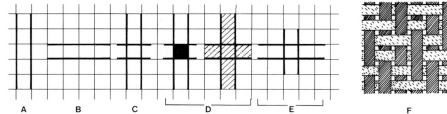

A   B   C   D   E

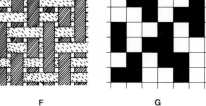

F   G

Weave notation.

Each horizontal line represents a shaft. And each vertical line of squares represents an end. A marked square is an end threaded in a particular shaft. The draft notation should be drawn directly above the weave notation so that the ends in the draft follow straight through into the weave.

When a weave construction is planned on point paper, the draft can be deduced from it by noting which ends have identical weft intersections and which are different. Ends with the same intersections can obviously be threaded on the same shaft, while each new variation will require a separate one. Thus if there are only four shafts on a loom, there are only four variations of the thread position in the draft.

To find the draft it is useful to number the ends, in the weave notation, starting with number one at the left-hand side and repeating numbers as intersections recur. Transfer the numbers to the draft in the form of crosses, starting with number one in shaft one, number two in shaft two, and so on, so that the marked squares will correspond to the threading position of each end. The highest number indicates the number of shafts required for this weave construction.

Pedal looms require a pedal tie-up plan and a pedalling order; dobby and table looms need a lifting plan. The notation for both sorts of shedding action are discussed and illustrated.

PEDAL TIE-UPS, PEDALLING ORDERS, AND LIFTING PLANS

Pedal tie-up and pedalling order for the counterbalanced loom

One of two methods of lam-to-pedal tie-up can be used for this type of loom (see page 28): either the full-pattern tie-up, or the single lam-to-pedal arrangement. The former is generally used for lengths of fabric; the latter makes it easier to design on the loom.

The symbols used here for the pedal tie-up and the pedalling-order notation are as follows. A dot in a cross represents a pedal attached to a lam and

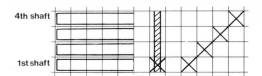

Draft notation.

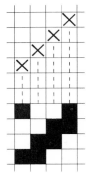

The draft notation should be drawn directly above the weave notation so that the ends in the draft follow straight into the weave.

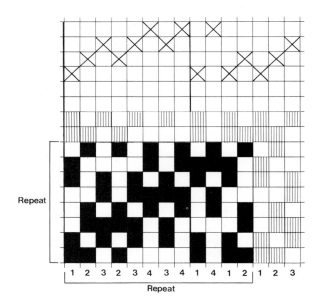

To find the draft, number the ends in the weave notation; the highest number indicates the number of shafts required for the weave. Transfer the numbers to the draft in the form of crosses; these will correspond to the threading position of each end.

hence to a shaft (see page 29). A blank square means that there is no tie-up with a lam. A dot by itself is a pedal pressed down.

FULL-PATTERN TIE-UP In this method, as the pedals are attached to the lams according to a prepared plan, only one pedal has to be pressed down to form each shed. With six pedals, just six different sheds are possible, but the pedalling sequence is unrestricted.

The notation for the pedal tie-up is placed to the right of the draft. Each vertical line of squares represents one pedal. And the horizontal lines represent the cords attached to each pedal, and correspond to the position of the shafts in the draft notation. Thus, a marked square is a pedal cord tied to a shaft (via a lam).

The pedalling order lies below the pedal tie-up notation, and is aligned with the weave notation. The vertical rows still represent the pedals, but each horizontal row now indicates a shed formation. The marked squares show which pedals should be pressed down (according to the pedal tie-up) to form the correct sheds.

It is important to remember that the counterbalanced shedding action pulls the shafts down, which contravenes a general rule that a mark in the pedalling or lifting plan represents a raised end. Thus the pedal tie-up plan is a reverse picture of the weave notation. This is most obvious when a straight draft and straight pedalling sequence are involved (as in the illustration right).

SINGLE LAM-TO-PEDAL TIE-UP Here each pedal is tied to one lam and therefore pulls down only one shaft. One, two, or three pedals may be pressed down simultaneously, which gives complete freedom in the choice of shed formation. When six pedals are available the two outside pedals can be tied up with the two sheds needed for plain weave.

The pedal tie-up is placed to the right of the draft, the pedalling order lies below it.

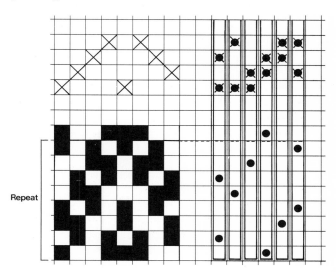

Full-pattern tie-up. Each pedal is tied up to several shafts in a predetermined pattern so that only one pedal has to be pressed down to form a shed with the required lifting order.

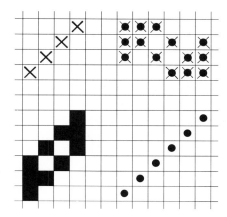

The counterbalanced shedding action pulls the shafts down, therefore the pedal tie-up plan is a reverse picture of the weave notation.

57

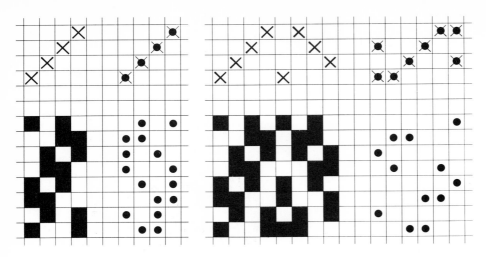

(*far left*) Single lam-to-pedal tie-up. As each pedal is tied to only one shaft, any pedalling combination can be used.

(*left*) When six pedals are available the outer two can be tied up with the two sheds needed for plain weave.

Pedal tie-up and pedalling order for the countermarch loom

The countermarch loom has two sets of lams so the pedal tie-up is different from the counterbalanced, and the symbols acquire a modified meaning. A spot in a cross here represents a pedal tied to a lower lam, i.e. a lifted shaft (see page 30). And a blank square is a pedal tied to an upper lam, or, in other words, a lowered shaft. Every square in the vertical pedal line thus shows a tie to one or other lam in a shedding unit.

The pedalling order notation is the same as for the counterbalanced loom pattern tie up. Only one pedal can be pressed down to form the shed. The number of different shed formations is limited to the number of pedals tied up, though they may follow each other in any sequence. This allows considerable flexibility and one pedal tie-up can be used for two entirely different weave constructions, as in the illustration, where, by changing the pedalling sequence, a pedal tie-up planned for a combined twill weave (see page 69) has been used to form a non-directional weave construction.

If the weave notation and the pedal tie-up plan are identical, the draft and pedalling order will both progress in an unbroken line.

When developing a cloth construction on point paper for a countermarch loom, the number of pedals required and the tie-up and pedalling order can be found by the same numbering method used to find the draft (see page 56). But this time number the shed formations. Start at the bottom of the weave notation with one and give a different number to each pick in the weave repeat with a different intersection sequence. Each of these numbers represents a pedal. The first horizontal pick line in the weave notation becomes the first vertical pedal line in the pedal tie-up, and so on. A dot placed in the square where the horizontal and vertical lines meet represents the pedalling sequence (see illustration right).

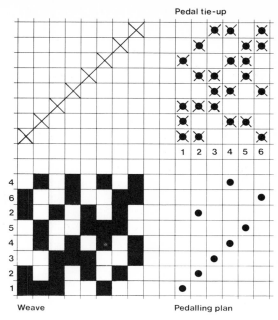

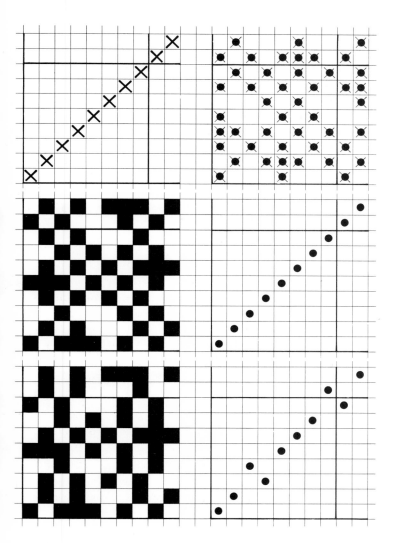

(*above*) The pedal tie-up and pedalling order can be found by numbering the shed formations in the weave. Each different warp/weft intersection sequence requires a pedal with an identical tie-up sequence.

Countermarch-loom tie-up. Only one pedal can be pressed down to form the shed, but by changing the pedalling order the same tie-up can be used for entirely different weaves.

59

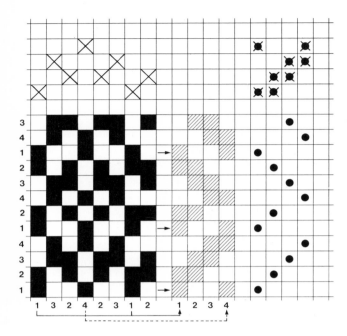

(left) To find the pedal tie-up when the draft is not straight, the weave construction must be condensed to one square for each end with a different weft intersection sequence.

(below) Split pedal tie-up. When two weaves that repeat on a different number of picks are combined in a stripe or check, the number of pedals can be kept to a minimum by dividing the tie-up into two groups.

When the draft is not straight, however, the weave notation has to be condensed to one vertical line of squares for each end with a different weft intersection sequence in order to deduce the pedal tie-up.

If the initial numbering of the picks results in an inconvenient pedalling sequence, the numbers can be rearranged so that the tied-up pedals lie in a different order. But the pedalling order must, of course, be amended as well.

SPLIT PEDAL TIE-UP When two weaves are used side by side (for example in a stripe or check) each with its own individual draft, and the weaves do not repeat on the same number of picks, the pedal tie-up can be divided into two groups. Each group of pedals serves one section of the draft, and two pedals – one from each group – have to be pressed down together for every shed. The pedalling order of one pedal group is entirely independent of the other.

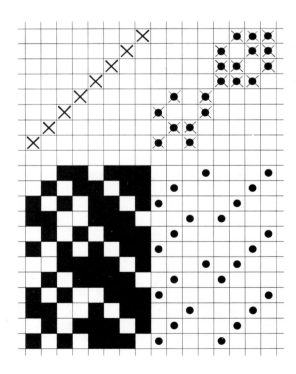

Dobby-loom lifting plan

Lifted shafts form the shed in the dobby loom. Each lag of the dobby chain represents a pick, and by the presence or absence of a peg controls the shaft movement (see page 36).

A spot in a square in the dobby lifting plan represents a peg placed in the lag, or in other words a raised shaft. The lifting plan is placed to the right of the weave notation, and a horizontal line of squares represents the lifting sequence of a pick on the same line in the weave notation. There is no lifting tie-up, of course, but to link the peg position to the shaft it controls, extend a horizontal line from the shaft and a vertical line up from the lifting plan, and mark the meeting point with a small dot. This helps to avoid relating a lifting sequence to the wrong shaft.

Each vertical row of squares represents the movement made by all the ends entered in the corresponding shaft. When the draft is straight, the weave notation and lifting plan are identical. If the draft is complex, the lifting plan again represents a condensed form of the weave construction (see opposite). By changing the draft, a variety of cloth constructions can be made with one lifting plan, and by changing the lifting plan, a variety of constructions can be made on the same draft (see illustration overleaf).

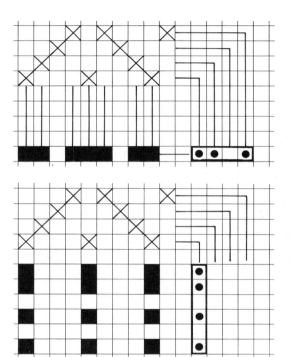

A dobby-loom lifting plan shows the position of the pegs in each lag. A horizontal line of squares represents the intersection of a pick; a vertical row represents the movement of all the ends in one shaft.

By changing the draft, a variety of cloth constructions can be made with one lifting plan.

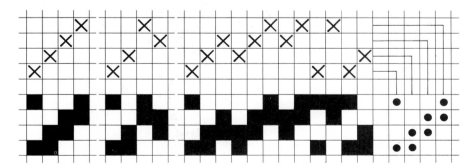

61

By changing the lifting plan, a variety of constructions can be made on the same draft.

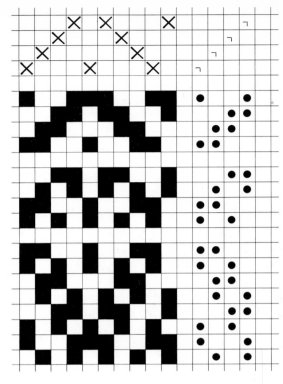

The lifting plan can be deduced by numbering each end in the weave with a different lifting sequence.

A Weave
B Repeat mark
C Numbering
D Draft
E Lifting plan for shafts 1 and 2

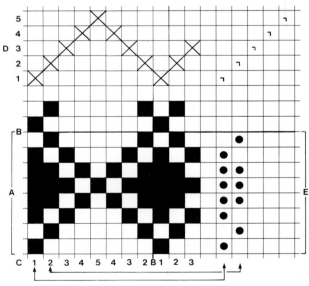

62

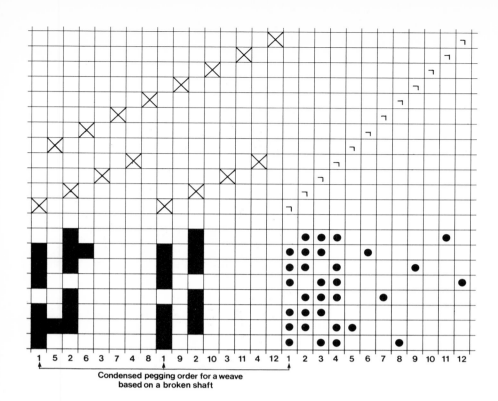

The weave construction can be worked out by the same method if the draft and lifting plan are known. The movement of the ends entered on shafts 1, 2, 5, and 6 is shown.

Condensed pegging order for a weave based on a broken shaft

To deduce the lifting plan of a weaving construction drawn on point paper, simply transpose the lifting sequence of each end attached to a different shaft from the weave notation into the lifting plan. Again, use the numbering method as described on page 56. In the same way, if you know the draft and the lifting plan you can work out the weave construction. But not, of course, if you have only one or the other.

Table-loom lifting plan

The lifting plan for a table loom is identical to that of a dobby because its shed is also formed by lifted shafts. However, as you need to be able to read the table-loom lifting plan very easily while pressing down the levers to make a shed, it is best to record the plan by numbers. If the levers are all on the same side of the loom, only one group of numbers will be necessary, but if they are on alternate sides divide the numbers into odd and even sets (see illustration).

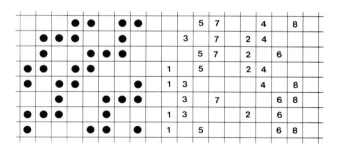

The table-loom lifting plan is numbered for convenient reading. If the levers that lift the shafts are placed on alternate sides of the loom the numbers should be divided into odd and even sets to correspond with the levers.

63

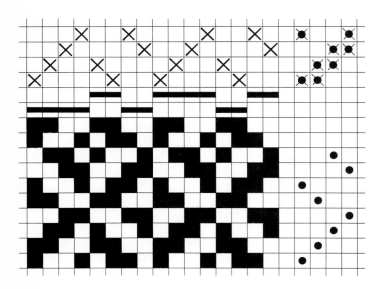

The reed notation is shown as a heavy broken line below the draft; each section of the line represents one dent.

REED NOTATION

The reed separates the warp ends between its comblike teeth and holds them parallel (see page 27). The reed notation shows how the ends are to be entered in the reed.

If the same number of ends are to be put in each reed dent right across the width of the warp, then the reeding instructions are simple and can be stated numerically. Thus if a reed with 32 dents per dm (8 per in) should have two ends in each dent, this information would be stated as 'Reed: 32 × 2 (8 × 2)'. The reed count always precedes the number of ends per dent.

However, if the end spacing is irregular, a full reeding plan has to be given for one repeat. Again the reed count precedes the reeding plan:

Reed: 48's (48 dents per dm) or 12's (12 dents per in).

Reeding plan:

|3|3|2|2|2|2|1|1|0|0|0|3|3|0|0|0|1|1|2|2|2|2|3|3|
= 38 ends in 24 dents, or 38 ends in 5 cm (2 in).

The reeding plan can be considerably shortened by eliminating repetitions of end numbers. The same plan would then be written as:

Reeding plan:

$$\underbrace{3}_{\times 2}\ \underbrace{2}_{\times 4}\ \underbrace{1}_{\times 2}\ \underbrace{0}_{\times 3}\ \underbrace{3}_{\times 2}\ \underbrace{0}_{\times 3}\ \underbrace{1}_{\times 2}\ \underbrace{2}_{\times 4}\ \underbrace{3}_{\times 2} = \begin{array}{l}38 \text{ ends in}\\ 24 \text{ dents}\end{array}$$

If the pattern of the weave is related to a specific reeding order, the reeding notation can be shown diagrammatically as a heavy broken line below the draft. Each bar represents one dent (see illustration), and stretches over the number of ends that are to be entered in it. (See also the example illustrated on page 139 in Gauze and Leno Fabrics.)

5 Basic weaves

There are three weave constructions upon which all other weave formations are based: the plain weave, which makes a firm, balanced cloth; the twill weave, which forms a directional line – the basis for all directional pattern formation; and the satin (reversed: sateen) weave, which forms a smooth, non-directional cloth – the basis for all equidistant patterns and for colour shading.

PLAIN WEAVE

Plain weave comes in many weights and qualities: muslin, hessian, calico, poplin, cheesecloth, and taffeta are a few examples. The plain-weave construction is uniform, based on a repeat unit of two ends and two picks crossing over and under each other in alternate order. Because the cloth has the maximum number of thread intersections, the cloth construction is very firm and the yarn requirement kept to a minimum. In fact, no other weave construction can produce a lighter cloth with the same stability, except a gauze weave.

The basic plain weave produces a balanced cloth with an equal number of ends and picks per centimetre (or inch). If the same yarn is used for both warp and weft, the vertical and horizontal yarn take-up will be identical. Warp and weft are used equally, and the same proportion of each appear on both sides of the fabric, forming a mosaic of texture and colour.

The maximum density of a square-set plain cloth is defined by the size of the yarn; the diameters of all the ends take up exactly the same space as the weft intersections between them. The number of ends and picks within a measured unit therefore increases in direct ratio to a decreasing yarn count (size) – providing the yarn texture remains the same.

Plain weave makes a non-elastic cloth. If the cloth's function requires elasticity it must be provided by the yarn (see page 12). Because plain weave has such a neutral construction the yarn's texture and character do not 'compete' with the weave, and so they determine the fabric's appearance and handle.

Plain-weave fabric can be woven equally well on a primitive loom or on the most sophisticated, yet, of all cloths, it is the most difficult to weave without faults. An irregular warp-tension control, a varying warp tension across the cloth's width,

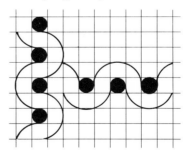

(*left*) A square-set plain weave.

(*above*) When the warp and weft yarn and the number of ends and picks are the same, the vertical and horizontal yarn take-up will be identical.

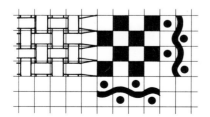

and variations in the degree of reed impact on the pick all result in a faulty cloth. And there is no weave pattern to disguise such defects as knotted yarns, spinning faults, variations in weft-yarn diameter, or patchy dyeing.

In theory all plain cloths can be woven on two shafts, but this is rarely possible in practice. For example, when the warp yarn is fine there are a large number of ends in the warp and the heddles (healds) would be too crowded on only two shafts. Therefore, for the sake of a good shed formation, and to keep friction to a minimum, four or even six shafts must be employed. Four shafts are often threaded in alternate order (1–3–2–4) so that they can be lifted in pairs.

Plain-weave variations

Although the plain weave construction is based on such a small repeat unit, it does lend itself to a considerable number of design variations by: (1) changing the end-to-pick ratio and yarn size (ribbed cloths and repp fabrics); (2) varying the thread density over a defined area (warp-and-weft spaced fabric); (3) extending the basic weave construction in one or both directions (hopsack weave); and (4) varying the warp tension (seersucker).

RIBBED CLOTHS Ribbed cloths are double-sided. Warp-faced ribs are formed by a high density of fine ends covering a straight thick weft. The rib runs horizontally across the cloth. Weft-faced ribs are formed by a coarse warp, sparsely set and highly tensioned, and a high density of fine picks. The rib is vertical. The cloth tends to be stiff and hard but can be improved by grouping several finer threads to make a thick one. The yarn tends to slip in weft-faced ribs unless they are very firmly woven.

(*right*) The handle of the cloth can be improved by forming the ribs from groups of finer ends or picks instead of from thick single threads.

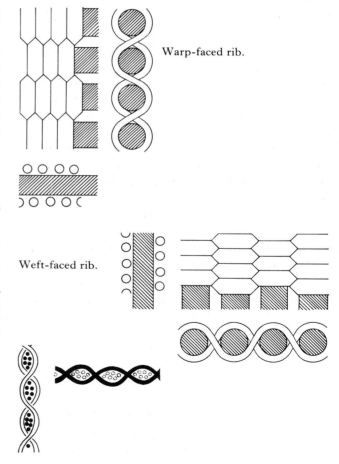

Warp-faced rib.

Weft-faced rib.

66

REPP FABRICS Repp fabrics are single-sided and of better quality than ribbed cloths. And although the horizontal ridge is prominent, it does not make the cloth's weight excessive.

The warp consists of alternate fine and coarse threads wound on to separate beams. Fine and coarse picks alternate, the fine picks passing below the fine ends, the coarse picks below the coarse ends.

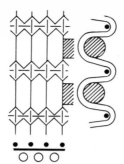

A repp fabric has alternate fine and coarse ends and picks.

WARP-SPACED FABRICS Numerous varieties of vertical stripes can be formed simply by changing the warp density. The area of change can be based on a small or a large repeat, or even extend across the full width of the warp. The change may be gradual or abrupt, subdued or pronounced, and since colour and texture are both affected by the ratio of ends to picks, a whole gamut of subtle changes is at the weaver's disposal.

While the effect of differential warp spacing has a strong visual impact, it tends to limit the functional use of the cloth. The maximum density of ends in a measured area is also limited by the need to form a clear shed opening; when too many ends are crammed into one dent they tend to stick together. The proportion of tightly packed to open areas depends largely on the cloth's purpose and on the quality and character of the weft. In general, firm yarns must be used for the weft to give the cloth its necessary crispness. The outer ends of a dense stripe will tend to move outward into the more open spaces. This tendency can be discouraged by using a fancy weft yarn – throughout or intermittently – between smooth picks. The texture of the fancy yarn helps prevent the warp thread movement.

WEFT-SPACED FABRICS In weft-spaced fabrics the scope for varying the pick density is limited. The change cannot be gradual because there is no sure way of controlling its regularity. In fact, any variation of reed impact is difficult on a hand loom. The mechanical cloth take-up of the power loom is an advantage here, because the speed of cloth take-up can be controlled to vary the pick density.

A combination of warp and weft spacing is well within the scope of a power loom. It can be done on a hand loom providing no regular pick density repeat is required.

SEERSUCKER CLOTHS The most effective seersucker stripes are made in firmly constructed, lightweight cloths. Two beams are essential, and the tension should be controlled by a friction brake. The fine ground warp has to be tight, the puckering warp slack, and the best results, i.e. regular pronounced puckering of the stripe, are achieved when an easer bar can be brought into action (see page 6). This holds the slack warp tight while the shuttle crosses the shed, and allows it to slacken when the weft is beaten in. The weft should be fine, since it does not form part of the visual effect. The seersucker texture is most effective if woven in narrow stripes.

A seersucker cloth can also be made by using two yarns with a different shrinkage. Only one beam is required, but the cloth should undergo a finishing process to gain full advantage from the shrinking differential. The seersucker effect is less pronounced in these cloths.

Weft seersucker effects can be made by weaving alternate stripes of soft and harsh straight yarns, or yarns that have a different elasticity, but the degree of puckering is limited.

HOPSACK WEAVES This weave construction is based on an extension of plain weave over two or more ends and picks. It may also be formed by a combination of different extended intersection units. To prevent ends from crossing over each other in the cloth, they should be entered in separate heddles on the same shaft. Even so, a slack end may tend to cross its partner in the weave intersection.

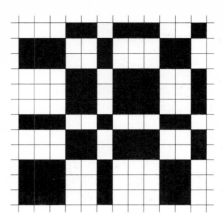

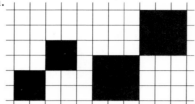

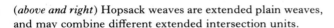

(*above and right*) Hopsack weaves are extended plain weaves, and may combine different extended intersection units.

(*below*) The angle of the twill is controlled either by the ratio of ends to picks, or by the length of the warp or weft floats.

TWILL WEAVE

All twill weave constructions are characterized by a diagonal 'twill line', though it may be more or less prominent. The line runs either to the right or to the left, and can be broken or reversed. The basic regular twill is formed by moving identical pick intersections progressively, over one end at a time, across the weave. Thus the repeat unit always has the same number of ends and picks whatever the size of the repeat.

A good twill cloth is softer and more subtle to handle than a plain weave; the yarn intersections are less frequent, which makes it more flexible. On the other hand a loosely constructed twill hangs badly, and when made into a garment will soon lose its shape.

The angle of the twill line is determined by the ratio of ends to picks in the weave construction. An equal number of ends and picks, as in the regular twill, produces a twill line at an angle of 45°. If there are twice as many ends the angle is increased to $67\frac{1}{2}°$, whereas twice as many picks decrease it to only $22\frac{1}{2}°$. Similar effects can be achieved by delaying the frequency of the pick's sideways step or by stepping the pick over more than one end. In both these cases there must be some plain-weave intersections between the twill to make a stable cloth.

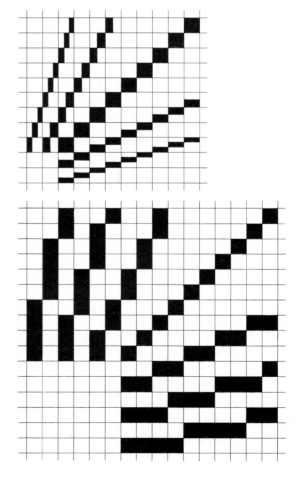

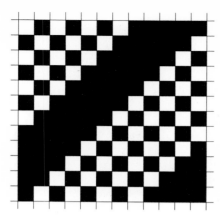

A band of plain weave between the twill floats will throw them into relief.

The twill's prominence depends largely on the density of the cloth construction and setting. For example, if broad lines of warp twill are divided by several plain-weave intersections, the warp floats will be thrown into relief by the pressure of the plain weave. The twill can be further emphasized if the warp yarn is twisted in the opposite direction to the line of the twill. Thus if the twill runs from left to right, the warp yarn should be twisted from right to left, i.e. in an 'S' twist. And ideally the weft should twist the same way as the twill – in this case from left to right, or in a 'Z' twist – but this is now often ignored as it involves keeping two stocks of yarn.

The pattern of regular twills can be recorded numerically. When each pick intersection is identical and the sideways progression of picks regular, it is sufficient to say that a twill is 2×2, or 3×3 (i.e. three ends lifted, three ends lowered). But with more complex weft intersections further details are necessary. For example: $T = \frac{2\ 1\ 1}{1\ 2\ 1}$ = 8 ends and picks in the repeat. Here 'T' refers to twill; the numbers above the line are the order of ends lifted, and those below it are ends lowered. If no other information is provided it can be assumed that the twill rises from left to right.

Though the minimum number of ends and picks required for a twill weave is three, the 2×2 repeat is usually considered the basic twill. This construction can vary in weight and quality between such extremes as foulard silk and Harris tweed.

Twill variations

The twill weave forms the basis of a great many diagonal design formations.

BALANCED TWILL The warp and weft floats are the same length, and the cloth is double-sided.

REGULAR WARP TWILL Has a preponderance of warp threads on the cloth face. The weft intersection advances continuously over one end at a time.

(*left*) Balanced. (*right*) Regular; warp preponderance.

REGULAR WEFT TWILL Has a preponderance of weft on the cloth face and again regular pick stepping.

COMBINED TWILL Warp and weft twills interchange in either a vertical or horizontal direction, or both.

(*left*) Regular; weft preponderance. (*right*) Combined.

 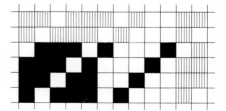

BROKEN TWILL The twill line advances in a broken line, either through a broken continuity of the draft or the weave.

BROKEN REVERSED TWILL Both twill and draft are broken and reversed at frequent intervals.

STEEP TWILL The pick's sideways step is delayed. Plain weave must be placed between the elongated warp floats to give the cloth stability.

DECLINING TWILL The opposite of steep twill; here the picks move successively forward over two or more ends at a time. Again plain weave is required to add firmness to the cloth construction.

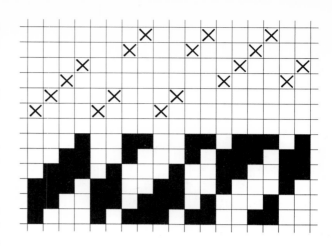

Broken.

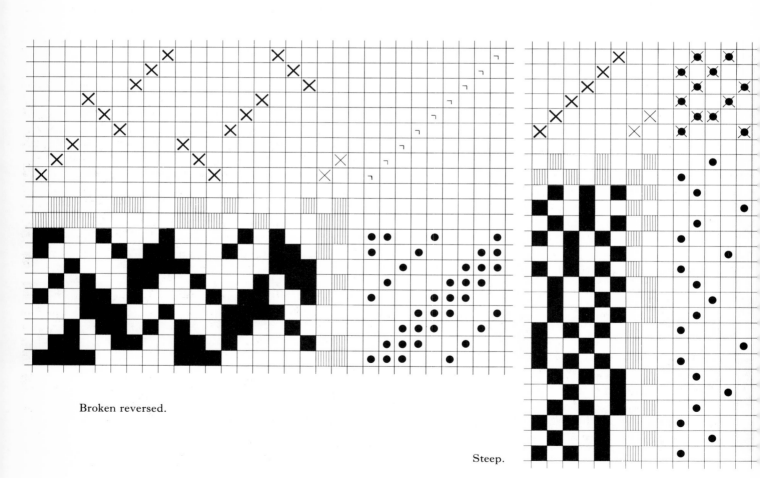

Broken reversed.

Steep.

INTERLOCKING TWILL Combines two twill weaves based on different repeat units. Usually alternate picks form one or the other.

UNDULATING TWILL An undulating twill line can be achieved in three ways:

1 By alternating the density of the ends in a measured unit to alter the twill's angle. The change of warp density is a gradual progression (see colour illustration on page 26).

2 By interrupting the draft sequence to affect the sideways step of successive picks. This method is only effective with a comparatively large number of shafts.

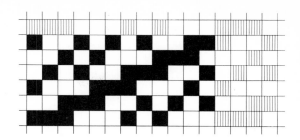

Declining.

(*right*) Interlocking.

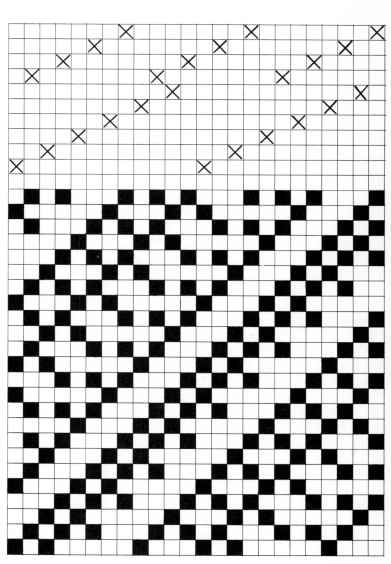

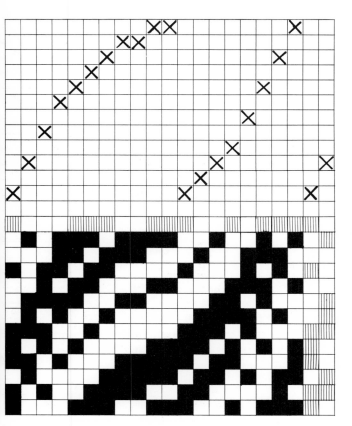

Undulating **2**, interrupted draft.

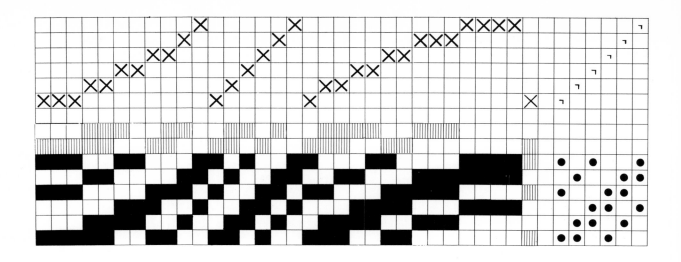

(*above*) Undulating **3**, varied number of ends per shaft.
(*far left*) Herringbone.
(*left*) Herringbone check.
(*below left*) Zigzag.

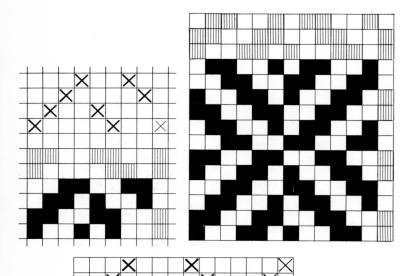

3 By varying the number of ends per shaft in a straight draft.

HERRINGBONE TWILL Basically this is a broken reversed twill, but at the point where the draft reverses one or more shafts are skipped depending on the number of ends and picks in the repeat. The reversing of the twill is thus clearly defined by the interchange of warp and weft floats. A true Herringbone can only be achieved with a balanced twill. A horizontal herringbone twill is formed on a straight draft; the lifting plan controls the twill direction and change.

HERRINGBONE TWILL CHECK A check is made by combining warp and weft herringbone. Care must be taken to form a clear dividing line at each change of direction.

ZIGZAG OR POINT TWILL By using a 'point' draft, i.e. a draft that reverses without a break, the twill line is made to run in a regular zigzag across the width of the cloth. Any twill weave can be used. A vertical zigzag is formed by changing the twill direction in the weave plan.

When planning a twill weave the designer should ensure that the twill runs regularly across the cloth. Even a broken or irregular twill has a regular progression of repeat units. To avoid any mistake it is prudent to extend the weave notation both upward and sideways beyond the repeat.

SATIN AND SATEEN WEAVES

Satin and sateen weaves form an unbroken cloth surface, the thread intersections being hidden as far as possible. Both weaves make a single-sided cloth and have an unbalanced warp-to-weft ratio.

The satin weave has a warp surface and a warp preponderance; the sateen weave has a weft surface and a weft preponderance. The weave notation is usually given as a sateen weave to save time. Satin weaves are frequently woven face down to keep the number of shafts to be lifted to a minimum.

Each end and pick intersects only once within the weave repeat. The points of intersection are called 'stitches' and should be equidistant. To find the stitching points within the repeat, divide

The contrast between satin and sateen surfaces in this cloth has been emphasized both by the colour variation and by the combination of a weft of coarse slub yarn with a fine warp. Photo: Wallace Heaton Ltd.

the total number of ends in the unit into two unequal groups. Each must contain more than one end, and the numbers must have no common denominator. For example, a repeat unit of eight ends and picks can only be divided into groups of three and five ends. The stitching points are therefore three or five picks apart over successive ends (see illustration). Other examples of satin/sateen weaves with a regular stitch distribution are: a five-end unit, which has two or three steps; a seven-end unit, which has three or four; a ten-end unit has three or seven steps, and a twelve-end unit has five or seven. A repeat unit of six ends and picks requires an irregular stitching distribution (see illustration).

Satin or sateen cloth has a soft handle and great pliability. The preponderance of ends over picks in the satin weave and picks over ends in the sateen hides the thread intersections. The unbroken surface this creates gives the cloth a high degree of lustre and the maximum amount of colour reflection. The infrequency of the weave intersections makes a dense cloth setting essential. And the greater the distance between the stitching points, the denser the cloth's setting must be to give it sufficient stability.

A sateen-weave notation forms a useful basis from which a great variety of non-directional weaves can be constructed. For example, crêpe weaves are mostly based on sateen (see page 95).

Shaded stripes changing from the weft surface of a sateen to the warp surface of a satin, are also based on the sateen notation. A horizontally shaded stripe can be made without increasing the number of shafts, and the shading may progress rapidly or slowly over an area. Vertically shaded stripes are developed on the same principle in a horizontal direction in the weave notation. But as each different end movement requires a separate shaft, this weave construction is beyond the capacity of a shaft loom and can only be woven on a jacquard.

When vertical stripes of satin weaves are combined with weaves with a more frequent inter-

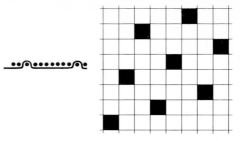

A repeat unit of eight ends and picks with the stitching points three picks apart.

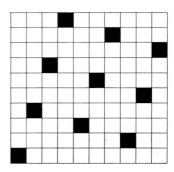
A five-end unit.

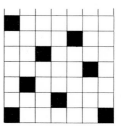
A ten-end unit.

A six-end unit has irregularly spaced stitching points.

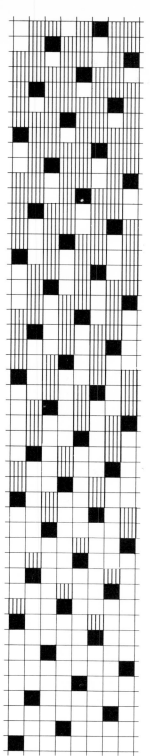

Shaded stripes changing from the weft surface of a sateen to the warp surface of a satin, based on the sateen weave notation.

section, two separately tensioned warps are necessary.

BASIC WEAVE COMBINATIONS

Interesting new designs can be developed by combining two or more different weave constructions in one cloth. For instance, by combining a weave with a warp preponderance with one of weft preponderance, different surfaces and colours are brought into play. When no colour is involved, such combinations will create purely textural changes. But if the yarns are dyed, the changing order of thread intersections will also affect their colour values. Stripes (both vertical and horizontal), checks, and simple isolated motifs all lie within the designer's scope.

To achieve a combination of weaves that is aesthetically satisfactory, it is usually important to have a clear dividing line between the weaves to prevent the threads slipping over each other. This is easy enough when the weaves are merely a reversal of each other – as shown in illustration 1, where a $\frac{3}{1}$ twill is joined to a $\frac{1}{3}$ twill, and in illustration 2, where a five-end satin is combined

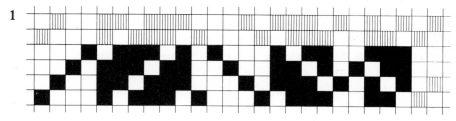

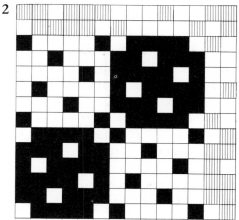

Clearly divided weave combinations. The textural contrast between warp-faced and weft-faced patterns can be emphasized when warp and weft yarns differ in character.

with a five-end sateen – because by reversing the weave construction a wft float is automatically placed against a warp float at the junction of the two weaves, thus preventing any thread movement from one weave to the next. A more complicated combination of a $\frac{2}{1}\frac{1}{1}$ twill with a five-end sateen is shown in illustration 3. Here the twill has two weft intersections (blank squares) within each repeat unit, while the sateen has only one warp intersection (solid squares). Hence as far as possible this one warp intersection has to be placed against one of the twill's weft intersections.

(*opposite*) Patterns formed by five weaves with identical warps and picking plans.

The use of different colours (or yarn textures) introduces a new design element: patterns can be created that are quite distinct from those formed by the weaves' construction. The coarser the cloth the more prominent the pattern.

3

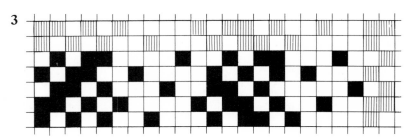

A combination of two basically different weaves: twill and sateen.

It may be far more difficult for the designer to find a clear dividing line when the two weaves to be joined have a different basic construction. For example, if a satin or sateen square is woven in a plain-weave ground, the size of the square may have to be slightly adjusted in order to place its stitching points against the correct plain weave intersection.

COLOUR AND WEAVE INTERACTIONS

When weaving with contrasting colours, the relationship between the weave construction and the warping and picking plan forms the basis from which many strongly patterned cloths can be designed. The series of illustrations opposite shows how five different patterns can all be woven on identical warps and with the same sequence of colours in the weft. The warping plan is: odd ends black, even ends white. The picking sequence is the same: odd picks black, even picks white. The visual effect of using this warping and picking sequence with any given weave construction can be established in graphic form as follows:

1 Record the weave construction (weave notation).
2 Mark the dark and light picks at the side and lower margins of the pattern diagram and draw faint lines through the squares occupied by black ends and picks.
3 Ignore the white ends and shade all the lifting points of the black ends only.
4 Ignore the white picks and shade all the squares where a black pick passes over an end.
5 Draw out the resulting colour pattern.

It is strongly advisable to work out such patterns beyond the repeat to ensure the next pattern repeat aligns correctly.

The series of illustrations overleaf shows how only one weave construction can produce a variety of patterns by the use of different warping and picking plans. The pattern is established by the same procedure.

When the repeat of the weave construction and the repeat of the warping and picking plan are not identical units, to show the full colour effect they must both be repeated until they finish at the same

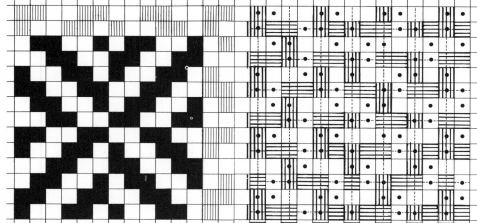

point. For example, if the warping and picking plan has a repeat of eight ends and picks, and the weave construction a repeat of six ends and picks, then the black and white colour pattern will repeat on twenty-four ends and picks, i.e. twenty-four is their lowest common denominator.

The process of deducing the colour pattern from a weave construction and warping/picking plan can be made far easier by using translucent colour. The method is as follows:

1 Mark the weave notation on point paper with small spots of waterproof ink. Repeat the weave notation as many times as is necessary to make a full repeat of the pattern plus a few extra lines beyond.

2 Paint the lines of squares that represent black ends and picks with a very light translucent colour – over the weave notation.

3 Where a black end is lifted, i.e. a spot under a tinted square, fill in the square with a darker translucent colour.

4 Where a black pick passes over an end, i.e. a blank under a tinted square, fill in the square with the same darker colour. The colour pattern is thus quickly established, and the weave construction is still visible through the translucent paint.

Colour-and-weave effects need not be confined to two colours or to basic weaves. Compound weaves used in conjunction with larger colour units of warp and weft will produce both bolder and more intricate designs.

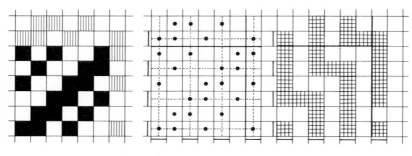

Patterns formed by the use of different warping and picking plans. The yarn size or texture can be varied instead of the colours.

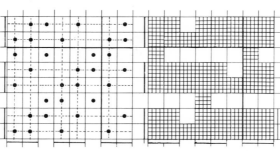

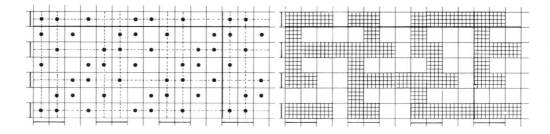

6 Compound weaves

All other weave formations are derived by either combining or extending the characteristics of the three basic weave constructions. They provide the basis for all structural modifications that can affect the pattern, texture or function of a cloth.

Although most of the cloth constructions and weaving methods discussed in this book can be woven on either a hand or power loom, a few – for example the warp and weft linkage techniques (see page 89) – can only be woven on a hand loom.

CORDED RIB CLOTH

Compared with the plain-weave ribbed cloths discussed on page 66 (formed from contrasting yarn sizes and tensions in warp and weft), the corded rib cloth has more pronounced ribs with deeper grooves between. The cloth's quality is superior and it has a better handle and wear performance.

Vertical corded ribs

The weave can be either a plain weave or a $\frac{2}{1}$ twill. Alternate ribs are formed by alternate picks. The first pick intersects the ends of the first rib and floats behind the second. The second pick intersects the ends of the second rib and floats behind the first; and so on (see illustration). Contraction of the floating picks when the cloth is taken off the loom and relaxes, pulls up the ground cloth into a

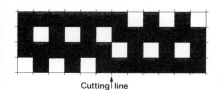

Cutting line

rib and forms a depression called the 'cutting line' where the alternate floating picks cross at the weave interchange. The rib's prominence depends on the degree of contraction. The width of the rib is generally limited to about 1 cm ($\frac{1}{2}$ in) because the weft contraction is not sufficient to pull a wider area of ground cloth together. The ratio of ends to picks is about equal in a plain-weave ground cloth; a $\frac{2}{1}$ twill will have a preponderance of ends over picks.

Bedford cords

These all have very clearly defined vertical ribs divided by deep cutting lines. The cords are usually woven in either a plain weave or a $\frac{2}{1}$ twill, while the cutting line is formed by a two-end unit

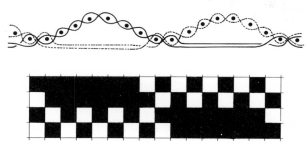

A plain-weave Bedford cord.

of plain weave (see below). The picks here alternate in pairs, but Bedford cords may also be woven with the floats alternating pick by pick as shown on page 80. Here the ground weave is a $\frac{2}{1}$ twill. The width of the cords can be varied to a certain extent – and different sizes combined in one design – but it is ultimately limited to the width of cloth that the weft floats can draw together.

A $\frac{2}{1}$ twill Bedford cord with the weft floats alternating.

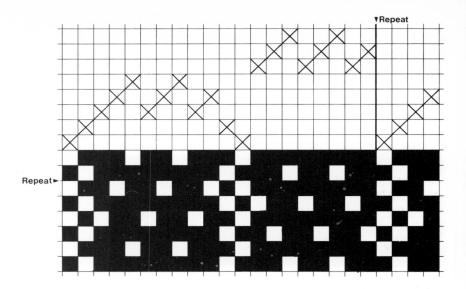

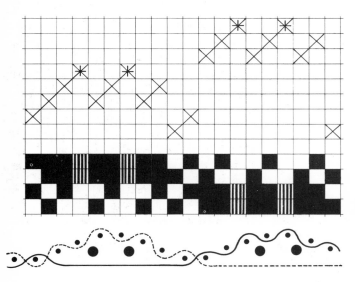

Wadding ends increase the prominence of the rib.

The prominence of the ribs can be increased by introducing wadding ends between the ground cloth and the floating picks. These are additional ends, and have to be entered on a separate shaft. Because they do not intersect but lie flat between the cloth and floats, there is no yarn take-up during weaving and they must be wound off a separate beam.

The wadding ends are threaded through the same dents as the ends of the ground cloth; their thickness is therefore limited by the reed density. If a widely spaced reed is used in order to accommodate thick wadding ends it will probably make reed marks in the ground cloth.

Horizontal corded ribs

A horizontal rib is made by turning the weave notation round through 90°. These ribs can be made very prominent because there is no limit to the thickness of the wadding picks. Vertical and horizontal cord weaves may be combined. But this precludes the use of wadding ends and picks. At least ten shafts are required to make a diagonal Bedford cord.

Worsted and woollen fabrics are particularly suitable for corded cloth constructions because

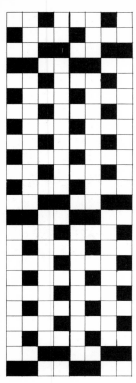

A horizontal cord.

Vertical and horizontal cords combined.
Each section of the draft and picking plan
is repeated four times.

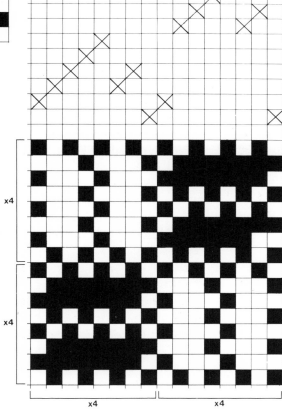

A diagonal Bedford cord always requires
a high number of shafts.

The stitching (or back) ends are a finer yarn than the ground warp, but must be strong to stand the high tension during weaving and to retain the welts when the cloth is in use. Wadding picks should be thick but soft, or they will make the cloth too stiff.

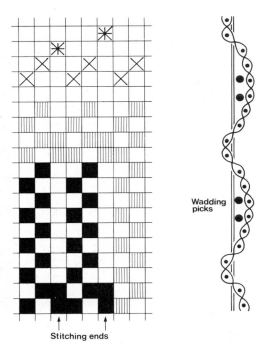

Wadding picks

Stitching ends

their finishing processes increase the shrinkage of the floating yarns and so increase the prominence of the ribs.

Piqué cloths

The characteristic feature of piqué cloths is that they consist of a firmly woven plain-weave cloth that has embossed lines running across the width. These lines may be straight or zigzag. With a jacquard loom more complicated patterns can be made. The ribs, or welts, are formed by an extra stitching warp, which intersects the old cloth by rising over one or two ground picks at points determined by the pattern. The stitching ends must be strong so that they can be highly tensioned in order to throw the ground cloth into relief. They are wound off a separate beam. The ratio of ground to stitching ends is usually two to one: each stitching end is placed between two ground ends in the reed.

The welt is emphasized by laying wadding picks between the cloth and the stitching ends. The stitching ends cross two consecutive picks at a time and therefore form an integral part of the design. This is particularly so in a waved piqué cloth where areas of ground cloth are divided by groups of stitching ends. The wadding picks curve round the outline of each stitched area, forming undulating relief lines across the cloth.

Piqué cloths can be woven without wadding picks; the tension of the stitching ends is sufficient to raise the ground cloth slightly.

WARP AND WEFT DISTORTION

Yarn distortions are created by juxtaposing areas with less thread intersection that can move closely together, with firm areas that have the maximum number of thread intersections. The degree of distortion depends on the weave combinations, the density of the setting, and the character of the yarn. Other forms of distortion can be produced by warp-tension differentials. Weft distortions require the reed impact to achieve the effect of the distortion.

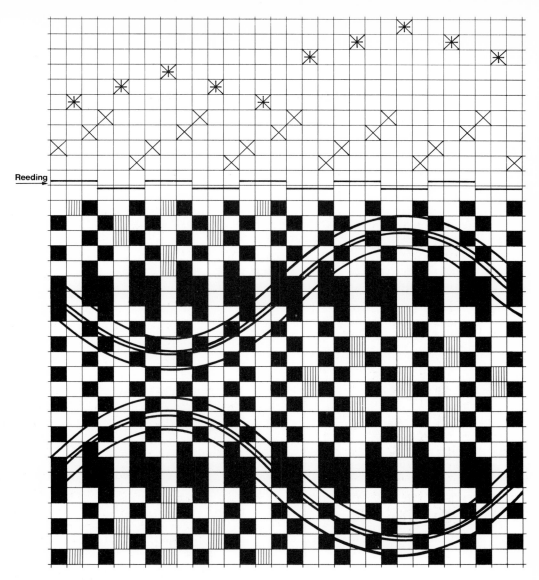

Reeding

To form a straight welt, all stitching ends are stitched into the cloth over the same two picks, hence only one extra shaft is required for these ends. More shafts are necessary to form a waved line (*above*). Recessed diamond shapes formed by the tightness of the stitching ends force the wadding picks out of the horizontal.

Warp distortions

The degree of warp distortion is somewhat restricted by the action of the reed, its function being to hold the ends parallel and at a preplanned distance from each other. Nevertheless warp distortions form an interesting design element with many applications.

GROUPED WARP DISTORTIONS Grouped ends between areas of plain weave are packed together by the firmness of the adjacent cloth. The distortion occurs where the groups fan out again into the plain weave. Several groups of bunched ends may be combined to make a repeat design. These distortions affect the translucency of the cloth by forming opaque areas where the ends are bunched.

SINGLE-END DISTORTIONS Single ends (N.B. these may comprise several threads) can be made to form a zigzag pattern through the length of the cloth. The distorting movements are caused by the alternate placing of weft floats (see illustrations). The distorted ends can zigzag in either direction and may be placed at any point along the cloth's width. The effect of this distortion does not become fully apparent until the cloth has been taken off the loom: the ground weave then contracts slightly increasing the sideways movement of the loosely held single ends.

The weft floats must not be placed too far apart

Grouped warp distortion.

Single line distortions. Photo: John Hunnex

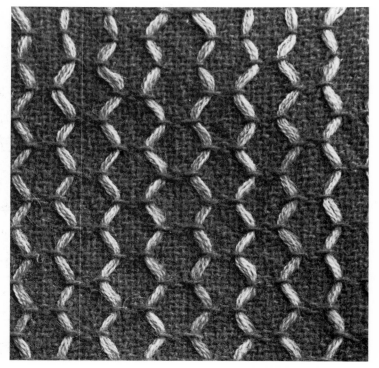

as they are the only picks holding down the distorted ends. Whether or not these extra ends will require a separate beam depends on the degree of distortion.

WARP DISTORTIONS MADE BY A FAN REED Fan reeds are fairly difficult to obtain now but can be made to order. They are almost twice the height of a normal reed. The reed wires are spaced in fan shapes; two examples are illustrated.

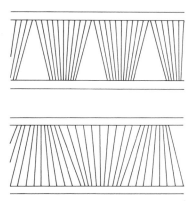

The warp distortion is achieved by raising and lowering the fan reed. The reed position can be changed at more or less frequent intervals. The upper section of the reed will both condense and spread out alternate groups of ends. The lower section of the reed will do this in reverse order. When the upper section is in position, i.e. when the batten is lowered, the shuttle has to cross the shed without the support of the shuttle race. It is easier to adjust the batten if the swords are suspended on pegs (see page 27). It may be necessary to drill extra holes in each sword to allow the batten to be raised and dropped sufficiently.

Plain weave is usually best for this form of distortion, though a gauze weave construction is also very effective. The yarn must be fine enough to pass through the dents at their closest placing. Rough yarns and yarns with little abrasion resistance are therefore not suitable.

A power loom requires a special batten to allow the reed to move up and down. The reed is in the normal position as the shuttle goes through the shed, and moves up or down to beat in the pick.

Weft distortions

Whereas warp distortions are diminished by the reed's action (except when a fan reed is used), weft distortions are increased by it. The reed's impact against the fell of the cloth affects the picks over two or three centimetres (about an inch) and packs together any that are not firmly held by warp intersections. It is well to remember that the effect of the beat is cumulative.

GROUPED WEFT DISTORTIONS The weave construction is as for a warp-distortion cloth, but placed horizontally: the groups of ends become groups of picks. Much wider areas of plain weave

Grouped pick distortion. Photo: John Hunnex

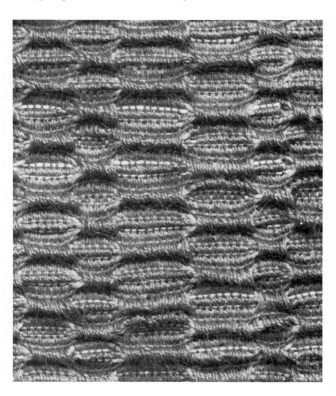

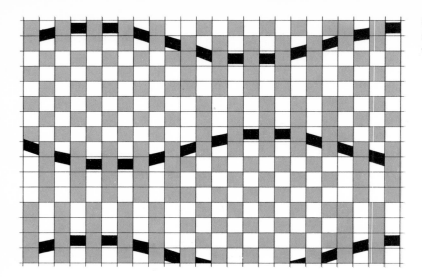

Single picks of a contrasting yarn introduced between the alternating densely woven areas emphasize the distortion.

can be used between the bunched picks and this will emphasize the distortion. The pick displacement can be further emphasized by outlining the distortion with single picks woven under the warp floats that group the picks together (see illustration above).

SINGLE-PICK DISTORTIONS Warp floats extending in opposite directions allow a single pick to zigzag across the cloth. The ground cloth should be fairly firmly woven, though not necessarily a plain weave construction.

WEFT DISTORTIONS MADE BY VARYING THE WARP TENSION Picks beat closer together when the warp is under a high tension. This can be exploited to distort a plain weave construction in the following way:

A warp – wound on one beam – is divided into alternate groups of ends, 'A' and 'B'. Each should occupy not less than 4 cm (1½ in) of reed space but may be much wider. The tension of the A groups and B groups is increased alternately, the effect being to pack the picks closely together in the highly tensioned groups and to spread them out in the slack ones. When the increased tension is changed from A groups to B groups, the pick density changes with it, but the even impact of

the reed allows the picks to adjust gradually.

The tension differential of the warp groups is controlled by two rocker sticks that extend across the width of the loom between the shafts and the back bar. They are held – about 15 cm (6 in) apart – by a pair of slats (see illustration) that are suspended from the top of the loom frame at the level of the heddle eyes. The A groups are placed over the first rocker stick and under the second, while the B groups go under and over.

Each rocker stick is connected to a pedal: 'AA' and 'BB'. By pressing down pedal AA, the back rocker stick tilts downward taking the A groups of warp with it, and the front stick rises lifting the same groups, thus increasing their tension. When pedal BB is pressed down the action is reversed.

This tension differential is only brought into action while the weft is beaten in. The tension should be normal for the shed formation and shuttle passage. The degree of tension variation can be controlled by the amount of pressure on the pedal. At the change of tension the pick is straight.

Cords attached from the rocker bars' suspension cords to the back loom posts prevent them from sliding towards the shafts.

The warp tension is more easily controlled on a width that does not exceed 90 cm (36 in).

86

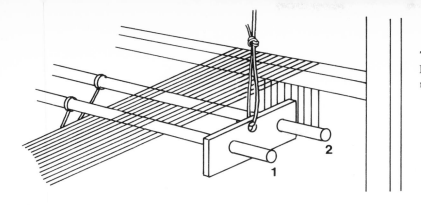

The tension differential of the A and B warp groups is controlled by two rocker sticks.

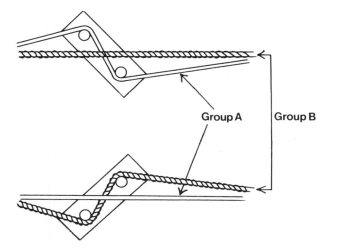

Group A   Group B

(*left*) Pressing down pedal AA tilts the rocker sticks backward, increasing the tension on the A ends. Pressing down pedal BB tilts them forward, increasing the tension on the B ends.

(*below*) Distortion by varying the warp tension is a technique most suitable for a plain-weave cloth. Here reed marks introduce a further design element – formed by leaving an empty dent between groups of four dents each carrying two ends. Photo: John Hunnex

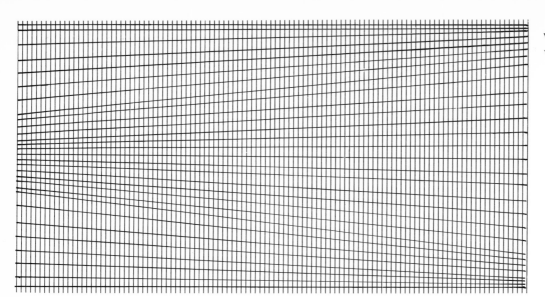

WEFT DISTORTIONS MADE BY VARYING THE
REED ANGLE The batten normally hangs parallel
to the breast bar, but as there is usually a series of
pivot points for its rocker bar the position can be
altered. By suspending the bar from a different
point on each side of the loom the weft will be
beaten in at a slight angle. When the rocker bar's
angle is reversed the angle of the weft changes
also. This distortion method varies the density of
the picks over the cloth's width, and forms a zigzag stripe across the fabric.

WEFT DISTORTIONS MADE BY OBSTACLES IN THE
FABRIC Bundles of yarn placed at random between
the picks during weaving, and removed after the
cloth has been finished, leave a permanent gap
between the picks (providing the cloth construction is reasonably firm). See colour illustration on page 51.

Combined warp and weft distortions

When small weave units in which the ends and
picks can move together are placed in opposition
to each other, i.e. warp floats against weft floats,
the result is a slightly perforated cloth. These
cloths are often called 'mock leno' because of their
superficial resemblance to the leno fabric. The

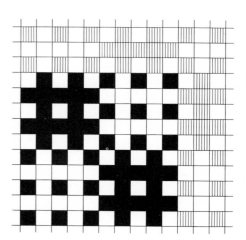

The mock leno cloth construction is based on a combination
of plain and hopsack weaves. The hopsack must have floats
that extend over an uneven number of ends and picks (three,
five, seven, etc.). The outer edge of the unit is plain weave.
The perforations occur where the weave units counterchange.

88

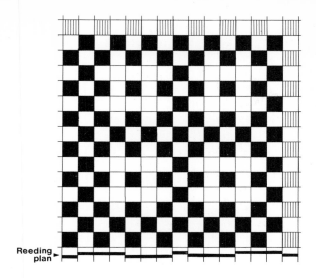

Reeding
plan ►

Separating the ends of each unit by a reed wire (as indicated in the reeding plan above), or even a dent, will increase the open appearance of a mock leno cloth.

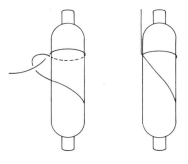

open appearance of the cloth is emphasized if the ends of each unit are separated by a reed wire, and even more so by an empty dent. Identical weave units – either warp floats or weft floats – must be separated by ends and picks intersecting in a plain-weave order to give the cloth stability.

WARP AND WEFT LINKAGE
Although the two weaving methods grouped under this heading have a weft that can be inserted by the shuttle, they require some hand manipulation, which interrupts the weaving rhythm and make them unsuitable for power looms.

Linked-warp technique
When a pick has been placed in a wrong shed it is usually taken out by throwing the shuttle back to the starting point. If the shed is not perfectly clear, the shuttle tends to catch on the wrong side of an end and if the caught end is loose, the pick may draw it out along the shed. This tiresome hold-up when unweaving can be made into an interesting design feature with many variations (see colour illustration on page 52).

This deflection of the ends is best seen in fairly open cloths with few textural features. The cloth construction demonstrated here is plain weave. All ends are incorporated into the ground cloth, but the ends that are to be made available for linkage must each be entered on a separate shaft. Two shafts are required for the ground cloth of this example, which leaves all remaining shafts for the linking ends.

The linking ends hang over the back of the loom and must be separately weighted. However, as the weight required is minimal, the weight of the bobbin holding the yarn is usually sufficient. As the yarn is taken up in the cloth more has to be released every time the bobbin reaches the back rest of the loom. It is therefore an advantage to wind the linking ends on selvage bobbins, which can be tensioned by a very sensitive friction brake and will dispense the yarn continuously (see

89

illustration right). These bobbins can be mounted on a creel placed behind the loom.

The weaving method is uncomplicated and is not limited by repeat requirements. A pick can only link one end at a time, but the frequency of linking and the selection of an available end is entirely unrestricted. The weaving sequence of the linked end illustrated is as follows:

1 Open the shed by lifting the second shaft. The first shaft and all shafts carrying independent ends are down. Throw the shuttle across the warp from left to right.

2 With the shuttle at the right side, lift one shaft carrying a linking end.

3 Throw the shuttle back to the starting point, catching the lifted end in its passage. As the shuttle emerges from the shed, stop the rotation of the bobbin. As the shuttle is pulled out farther, the linked end is pulled through the open shed. When it has reached the desired position close the shed.

4 Beat in the pick and hold the batten against the fell of the cloth while the shed is changed, locking the linked end into position.

5 Push back the batten and the next pick can be inserted. The linked end has been diverted to the left. When the shuttle starts from the right side, the diversion of the linked end is to the right.

Wherever the shuttle has been returned to the starting point with a linked end, the cloth will have a double pick, the frequency of this depending on the frequency of the warp linkage. The double picks can be made less noticeable if double ends are also distributed irregularly across the warp.

It is possible to divert several ends with one pick if they are grouped together.

Linked-weft technique

At first glance linked-weft cloths appear to have been woven with a tapestry technique. However, a closer inspection will show that all picks that change colour or texture at a point between the two selvages are in fact double picks (see colour

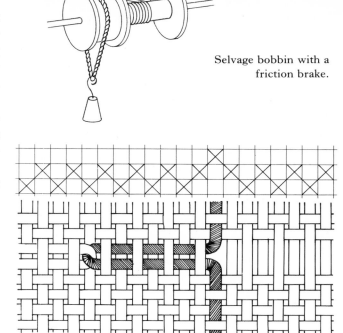

Selvage bobbin with a friction brake.

Linked-warp technique.

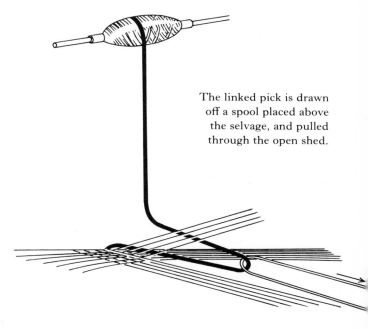

The linked pick is drawn off a spool placed above the selvage, and pulled through the open shed.

90

illustration on page 101). This is the clue to the weaving method. One of the picks is carried by the shuttle, the other is drawn off a spool placed beyond the selvage. Plain weave is generally used for the cloth construction, but the technique lends itself to many other weave constructions.

Attach a metal rod or piece of wooden dowelling to the loom frame above the selvage, extending forward toward the front of the loom above the shed opening. Place a spool of yarn on the rod and secure the thread at the selvage. Throw the shuttle through the shed from the opposite selvage, pass it behind the linking yarn and, without changing the shed, throw it back to its starting point. As it is caught, restrain the spool from further rotation. With the shed still open pull the linked thread along to any point between the selvages, according to the design (see illustration opposite). Change the shed ready for the next pick insertion. The weight of the yarn on the spool usually provides sufficient tension for the linked pick, to correspond with the tension of the pick from the shuttle.

Spools providing threads for linking may be placed above each selvage, and brought into action at different stages, but they cannot be linked by the same pick. This weaving technique has design limitations in that all shapes must spring from the selvage.

However, by changing the weaving method slightly, linked threads can be pulled into the cloth from either side by the same pick. Push the shuttle into the open shed at the point where the central colour begins in the design (see illustration), and bring it out at the right-hand selvage. Pass the shuttle behind the linking thread and throw it back across the same shed to the left side of the warp. Pull the linked thread into the required position, pass the shuttle behind the left-hand linking thread and reinsert it in the same shed. Take the shuttle out of the shed at the point in the design that forms part of the central motif (indicated by a dotted square). Pull the left-hand linking thread into the required position. Change the shed, reinsert the shuttle in the new shed two ends farther along from where it was taken out, and push it through the remaining part of the warp.

TEXTURE WEAVES

Without using fancy or textured yarns, or a differential warp tension, few weave constructions will produce a fabric that has a prominent texture. But three good examples are the honeycomb, Brighton honeycomb and crêpe weaves.

Linking threads can be pulled into the cloth from either side by the same pick. The point at which the shed is changed should be varied to conceal the longer float produced, unless this is to be used as a design feature.

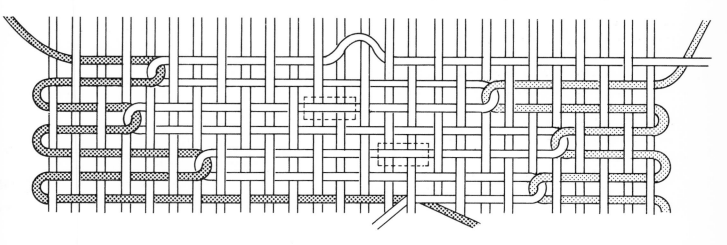

The honeycomb weave

This weave construction produces a textured fabric by the contraction of long floats of warp and weft after the cloth has been taken off the loom. These warp and weft floats form four sides of a square. When they contract the square's centre is forced inward making a 'cell'. The cloth is double-sided, and on the reverse the floats extend between the central points of the face squares, so their contraction serves to emphasize the texture on the face by increasing the depth of the cells.

The weave construction is based on a single-stitch diamond weave: diagonal stitching lines divide alternate rows of diamond shapes filled with warp or weft floats. This basic honeycomb weave remains the same however many ends and picks in the repeat unit, but the setting should be increased with the length of the floats. A cloth with a large repeat can be made firmer by doubling the stitching lines.

All honeycomb weaves are woven on a point draft. The smallest repeat unit is on six ends (requiring four shafts), but this does not produce a very pronounced texture.

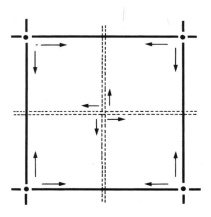

The cloth is double-sided. If a coarser yarn is used to outline the squares on one or both sides of the cloth, the effect is emphasized.

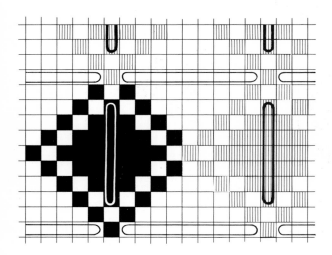

Honeycomb weave. The prominence of the texture will be increased by a yarn with a greater degree of shrinkage.

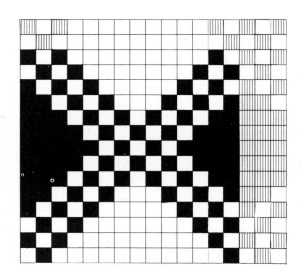

Double stitching lines make a firmer cloth.

The Brighton honeycomb weave

The texture of this weave is less regular and makes a more interesting cloth than the honeycomb construction. It is single-sided, the reverse side having a less prominent texture.

The Brighton honeycomb weave requires a straight draft. The smallest repeat unit is on eight ends and picks. Increases in the repeat size must be by multiples of four, i.e. twelve ends, sixteen ends, etc.

The weave is based on a combination of both double and single diagonal lines enclosing diamond shapes that each contain four smaller diamonds: two of warp floats and two of weft. The longest warp and weft floats form ridges that force down the centres of the squares on either side. These squares are formed alternately by the crossing of the stitching lines and by the meeting points of the warp and weft diamonds. The cells formed by the stitching lines are slightly larger than those formed by the centre of the warp and weft diamonds.

Each diamond-shaped area divided by the stitching lines encloses two warp diamonds and two weft diamonds.

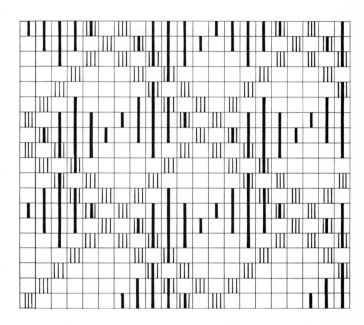

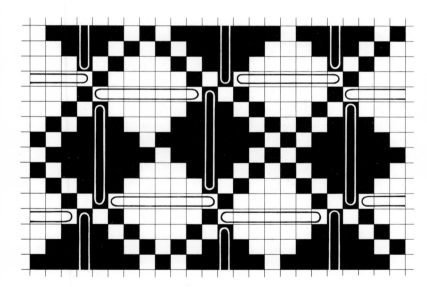

Because the Brighton honeycomb is one-sided, it has pairs of ends and picks which act alternately to form the cells.

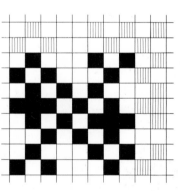

The smallest repeat unit is on eight ends and picks.

93

Crêpe weaves

All crêpe fabrics have a non-directional weave construction, which is broken up by short floats; the effect produced is a confused textural pattern. There are the same proportion of ends and picks on the cloth face and the fabric is often square set.

Crêpe weaves are usually developed by adding extra stitching points to a basic sateen weave. Alternatively stitching points can be added or eliminated from a plain-weave base. Four examples:

1 A crêpe weave based on a crow sateen.

2 A crow sateen weave and a $\frac{1}{3}$ twill combined. The twill runs from right to left.

3 A weave construction based on plain weave with equal number of stitches added.

4 A crêpe weave formed by rotating a small motif round a centre point.

BACKED CLOTHS

The addition of backing threads is a way of providing a cloth with the weight, strength, or stability necessary for its function without interfering with the aesthetic appeal of its construction. These extra threads may be either ends or picks. They lie behind the face cloth and are woven into it at regular intervals.

Warp-backed cloths

These fabrics have two sets of ends and a common weft; the ratio of 'face' to 'backing' ends depending on the reason for the backing and on the yarn count. Since the backing ends are purely functional their intersections must be concealed as far as possible, and they are generally woven into the face cloth between adjacent face-end floats. This is easier to do when the face cloth is woven from coarse yarn and the backing ends are fine (adding

(*opposite*) The Brighton honeycomb weave causes considerable cloth contraction, which can be emphasized by combination with a firmer weave. Photo: John Hunnex

Crêpe weaves.

1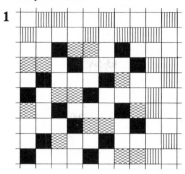

2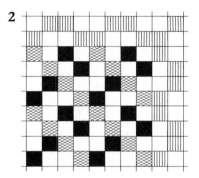

3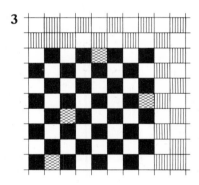

4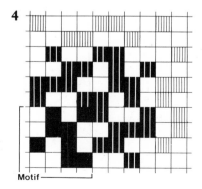

Motif

strength not bulk). The amount of interweaving necessary depends on the purpose of the backing. If the ends are to add weight they may be left floating fairly loosely at the back, but if they are to add stability and to support the construction of the face weave then they must be firmly interwoven. When the face and back ends have a different yarn take-up they must be run off separate beams.

The step-by-step development of a warp-backed weave construction where the ratio of face to backing ends is two to one, is as follows:

1 Draw out the weave construction of the face cloth.

2 Place the backing ends, one between each pair of face ends.

3 Enter the face weave in the blank lines between the backing ends.

4 Place the mark where a backing end is to be raised over a pick between two warp floats of the face cloth. The vertical cross-section shows the relationship between face and backing ends. They require separate shafts.

5 Reduce the lifting plan to basic symbols.

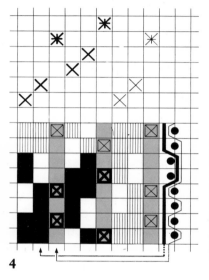

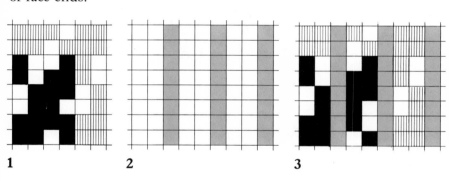

1 **2** **3** **4**

Construction sequence of a warp-backed cloth.

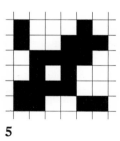

5

Reversible warp-backed cloths

These cloths are double-sided; the face and reverse may be the same or have different weave constructions. When constructing a reversible cloth on point paper it is essential to remember that in the weave notation the back cloth must be planned in reverse, because you are looking at

96

Construction sequence of a
reversible warp-backed cloth.

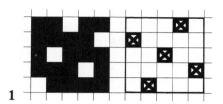

1

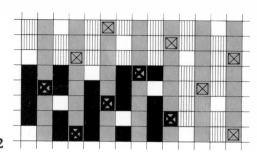

2

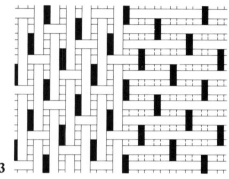

3

it from the front of the fabric through the face
ends. Thus if a cloth is to have satin weave on both
sides, it must be planned with a satin face and
sateen reverse, or the back cloth will be woven
upside down. The construction of such a cloth
with an equal number of face and back ends is as
follows:

1 Draw out the face and back cloth weave constructions.

2 Place the back and face ends alternately.

3 Hide the back-end intersections between face-
end floats.

The same principles apply if the face and back
cloths are different; the weave notation for the
back cloth must be drawn on point paper in
reverse. The example illustrated has an eight-end
satin on the face and a $\frac{3}{1}$ broken twill on the
reverse; therefore the back cloth is drawn as a $\frac{1}{3}$
broken twill in the weave notation.

Once the method of constructing a warp-backed
cloth is understood, a condensed weave notation
can be used to find the best positions for the backing ends and stitching points. This is a particularly useful system when the face cloth has a
complicated weave construction.

The weave notation shows only the ground
weave (see illustration overleaf), which is indicated
by thick vertical lines drawn in the centre of the
squares. The dividing lines represent the backing
ends. When the position of the backing ends has
been worked out mark them at the bottom of the
weave notation, and then fill in the lifting points
between the face ends. The draft and lifting plans
are established in the usual way (see system on
page 56).

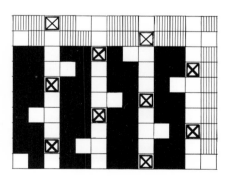

A reversible warp-backed cloth with the face ends woven in
an eight-end satin and the back ends in a $\frac{3}{1}$ broken twill,
the ratio of face to back ends is two to one.

97

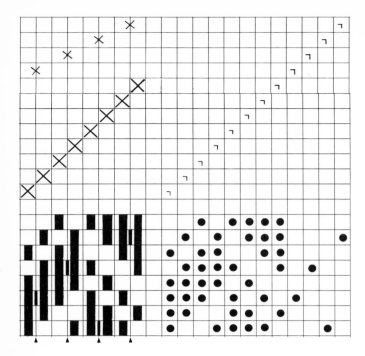

A condensed weave notation shows clearly the best positions for the back-end stitching points between the face-end floats.

Weft-backed cloths

Weft-backed cloths have a common warp and two wefts – although if the wefts are coarse they may not necessarily have a great preponderance of picks over ends. Though very similar in appearance to the warp-backed cloths, the advantage of these cloth constructions is that they need only one warp and therefore require fewer shafts to weave them.

Their construction follows the same principles as the warp-backed fabrics: the back pick passes over an end between weft floats of the face cloth. The yarns used for the weft can be soft and full. The construction of a cloth woven with two face picks to one back pick is as follows:

1 Draw out the weave construction of the face cloth.

2 Mark the position of the backing picks: because they lie below the ends they are marked with dark hatching (indicating raised ends). An end dropped below a backing pick is shown by a circle.

3 Combine the face weave and backing picks.

4 Reduce the lifting plan to basic symbols.

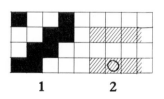

The construction sequence of a weft-backed cloth. The final stage shows the pegging plan for dobby lags.

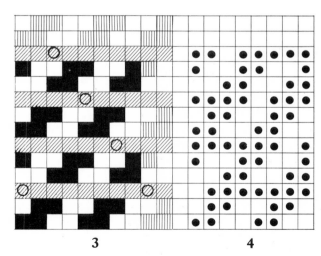

The same condensed method can be used to develop weft-backed cloths on point paper (see page 97). But because each backing pick lies below most of the ends the weave notation may be more confusing than for the warp constructions, and some designer/weavers prefer to reverse the symbols – using blank squares for warp over weft, and marked squares for weft over warp. The illustration shows a weft-backed cloth constructed by this method. When pegging the lags or tying up the pedals the notation must be reversed, unless, to avoid lifting too many shafts, the fabric is to be woven face down.

Warp-and-weft-backed cloths

These fabrics must not be confused with double cloths (see page 103), the backing threads do not form a distinct cloth layer. The principle of stitching the backing threads into the face cloth is again exactly the same as for the warp-backed and weft-backed cloths. And the condensed method of developing the weave construction is a considerable advantage here. The illustration below shows a diagram of a warp-and-weft-backed cloth with a ratio of two facing ends and picks to one backing end and pick.

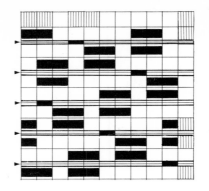

The condensed method showing the weave in reverse.

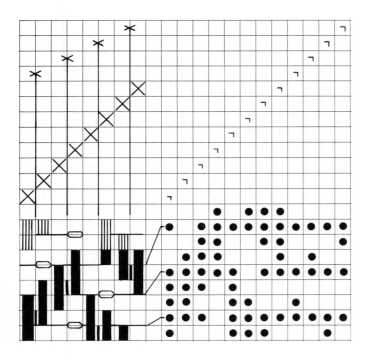

Although the diagram of the weave is condensed to find the stitching points for the backing ends and picks, the lifting plan gives equal importance to each end and pick.

99

7 Multilayer cloths

As the name suggests, these compound fabrics are composed of two or more cloth layers, each of which is a distinct fabric with its own warp and weft and requiring its own set of shafts. The cloths may be stitched together at various points, joined only by a central row of stitching (see colour illustrations page 102), or completely interchanged; the method chosen will of course depend on the fabric's design and purpose. Any of the methods may be combined.

The basic methods of stitching or interchanging the layers:
1 A face end is dropped below a back pick.
2 A back end is lifted over a face pick.
3 A central stitching end intersects the face and back cloths alternately.
4 A central stitching pick intersects the face and back cloths alternately.
5 A face pick passes under a back end.
6 A back pick passes over a face end.
7 The two cloths are interchanged horizontally.
8 The two cloths are interchanged vertically.

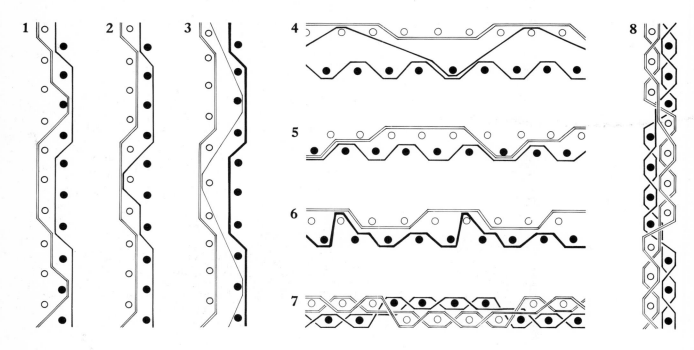

(*opposite*) Linked-weft design based on linkage extending from both selvages. Although only three colours can be used across the width of the cloth at a time, the design can take any form and is not limited by either the draft or the lifting sequence. The cloth is made from roughly spun linen yarn.

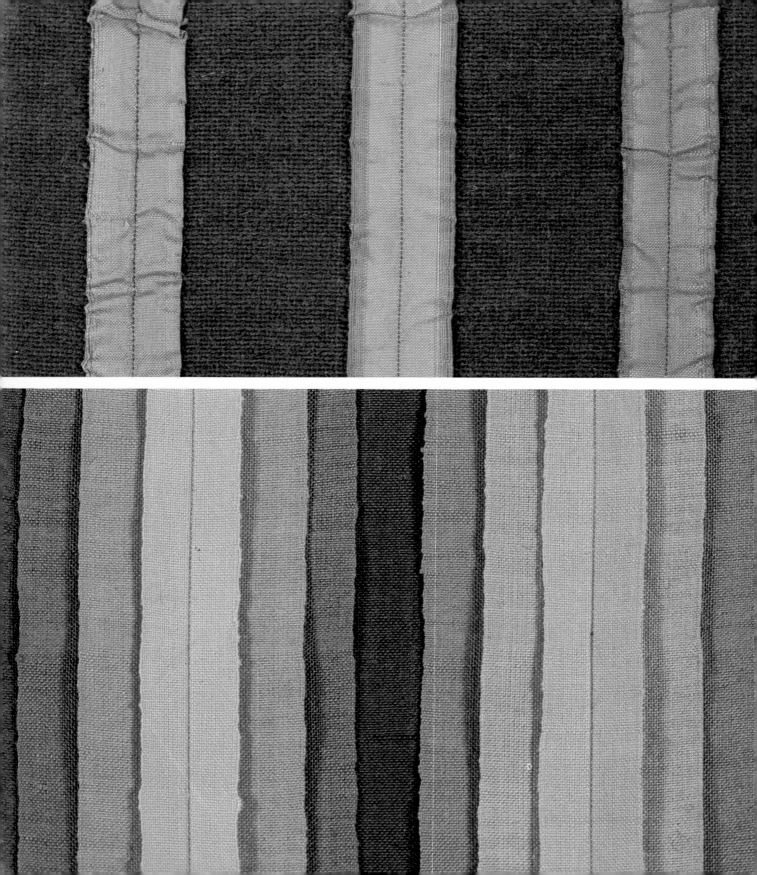

○	The light ends and picks.
•	The dark ends and picks.
▨	All back ends and picks (the blank squares represent the face ends and picks.
■	Face-cloth weave, warp lifted.
	Face-cloth weave, a face pick passes over a face end.
▨	Back-cloth weave, warp lifted.
▦	Back-cloth weave, a back pick passes over a back end.
⬤	The back pick passes under a face end, the face end is lifted.
▥	The back end is lifted over a face pick.
◉	The face end is dropped below a back pick.
▨	Ends and picks in the central layer (for treble cloths).
▦	A centre end lifted (for treble cloths).

1
Face weave   Back weave

(*opposite*) Multilayer cloths. The superimposed bands of cloth are interwoven by a central row of stitching. The puckering effect (top) is caused by a slight tension differential between the warps of the two cloth layers. Cloths designed and woven by Alison Howells.

The double-layer cloth construction is the most common of the multilayer cloths and has many applications, for example:

1 A backing cloth can give stability to a face cloth that has been loosely constructed in order to display the character of the yarn.

2 Two cloths can be interchanged as a feature of the design.

3 'Blister' (puckering) cloths can be made by combining cloths with different shrinking properties.

4 A reversible cloth can be made by combining two cloths with different colours and/or textures.

5 A tube can be woven by joining a double cloth at both sides.

6 A single cloth of double width can be made by weaving a double cloth joined at one side.

BASIC DOUBLE-CLOTH CONSTRUCTION

The basic method of constructing a double cloth applies to the most complex constructions. The weaver has to make three decisions: First, the weave construction of each cloth. Second, the setting of the face cloth, i.e., the ends and picks in a measured unit. Third, the ratio of face-cloth ends and picks to those of the back cloth. (This establishes the setting of the back cloth.)

These three factors are interrelated and cannot be considered independently.

If the two weave-repeat units of each cloth are not identical, the smaller unit must be repeated until it coincides with the larger.

The basic step-by-step construction is as follows:

1 Draw out the weave constructions of the face and back cloths. (It is advisable to use watercolours or translucent paint in contrasting colours to distinguish the notation of the two cloths. Here, symbols are employed and all the cloth constructions illustrated have a light-coloured face cloth and a dark back cloth.) Decide the ratio between each cloth's ends and picks.

2 Mark the position of the face and back ends and picks to the left and below the weave notation according to the ratio chosen. (In this case the ratio is one to one.)

3 Lightly indicate the squares representing back ends and picks. A light translucent yellow is best if colour is used.

4 All face ends have to be lifted when the back pick is inserted. Mark these lifting places.

5 Mark the face weave where a face end is lifted over a face pick.

6 Mark the back weave where a back end is lifted over a back pick.

7 Reduce the weave notation to basic symbols.

The vertical and horizontal cross sections show the two cloths lying on top of each other but not joined.

The draft is found by the usual numbering system (see page 56). Some weavers like to place the face and back ends in separate groups of shafts, others prefer a straight draft.

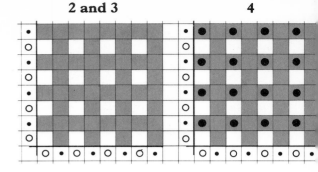

STITCHED DOUBLE CLOTHS

There are two methods of stitching the cloths together: a face end is dropped under a back pick, or a back end is lifted over a face pick. Both methods can be used together if the two cloths need to be firmly stitched. The stitching inter-sections (see page 100) are rarely used as part of the design but are concealed as far as possible between long floats of thread.

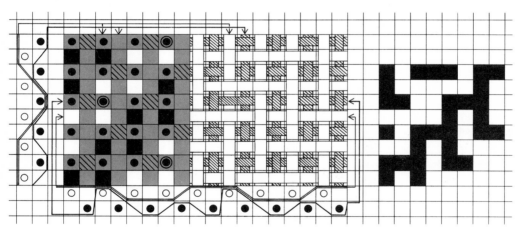

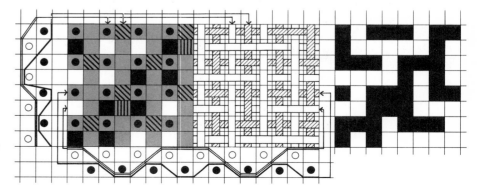

Stitched double cloths.
(*above*) A face end dropped under a back pick, (*right*) a back end lifted over a face pick.

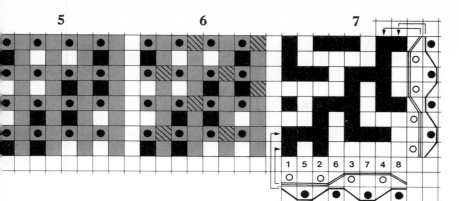

Basic double cloth construction sequence.

If the cloth is to be reversible, the stitching points should be hidden on both sides (see illustration below). When planning the reverse side it must be remembered that the weave notation shows the back cloth from behind.

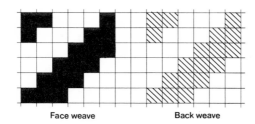

Face weave   Back weave

A double cloth with a 3 × 3 twill weave for both layers. At X a back end is lifted over a face pick between warp floats of the face cloth, while at Y a back pick passes over a face end between weft floats of the back cloth. Thus the stitching points are concealed in both cloths.

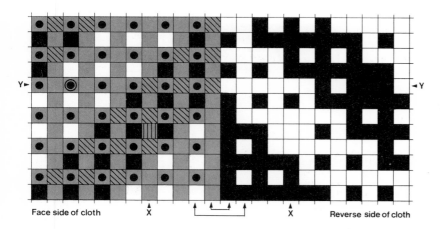

Face side of cloth   X   X   Reverse side of cloth

The draft is not affected if the stitching point occurs regularly in each repeat unit. But if it only occurs in certain units the 'stitching end' must be carried on a separate shaft.

CENTRE-STITCHED DOUBLE CLOTHS

The two cloths are held together by extra ends or picks, caught alternately in the weave of either cloth (see page 100). The threads used are usually fine and strong, and remain hidden between the layers. Any two cloth constructions can be joined by this method.

Centre-stitched ends

These ends are alternately raised over a face pick and dropped under a back pick to bind both cloths together. The frequency of this alternate stitching depends on how firmly the cloths must be attached. The stitching points should be concealed between long floats of warp or weft. The double cloth illustrated is formed from two 2×2 twill cloths. Every ninth end is a stitching end. The stitching ends require one or more extra shafts. Because they are fine and lie comparatively straight in the cloth, they must be separately tensioned, and so are carried on a second beam.

The construction sequence of a double cloth with centre-stitched ends. Each cloth is a 2×2 twill weave, the stitching end is marked at S. The spacing of the stitching ends and the number of stitching points depends on the character of the double cloth and on its function.

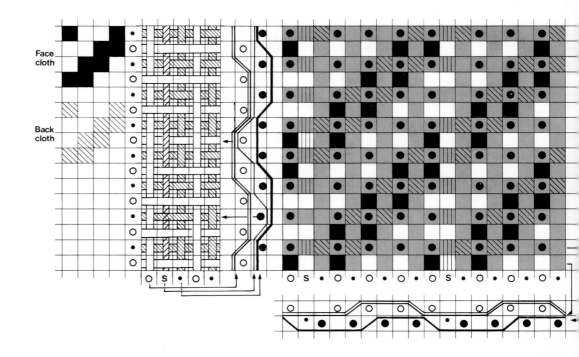

Centre-stitched picks

If a second beam is not available, the two cloths can be attached by stitching picks. The example illustrated shows a face cloth with a 2 × 2 twill construction, while the back cloth – in the notation – has a four-end broken sateen weave (also known as 'crow twill'). On the reverse side of the cloth this will be seen as a four-end broken satin weave. Every ninth pick is a stitching pick. The stitching pick is woven into the face cloth by lowering a face end, and into the back cloth by raising a back end. In the face cloth the pick lies between weft floats; in the back cloth it also lies between weft floats in the weave notation, but appears between warp floats when the cloth is turned over.

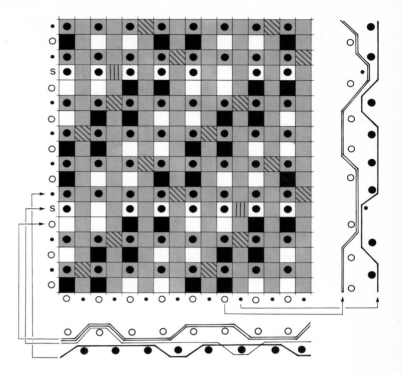

Centre-stitched picks: the face cloth is a 2 × 2 twill, the back cloth a four-end broken sateen weave. The stitching picks can be introduced at any distance from each other, but the distance between stitching points is controlled by the size of the draft.

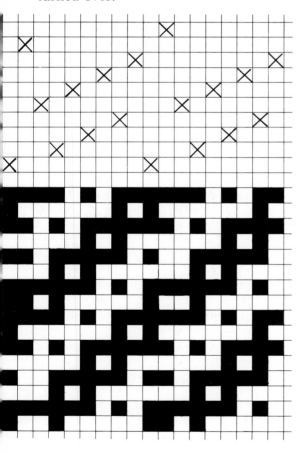

107

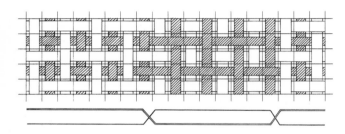

Vertical cloth interchange.

A weft only interchange.

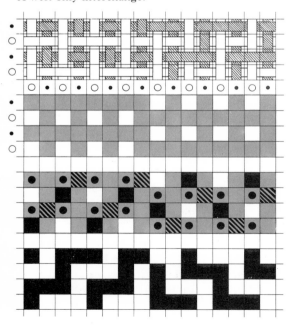

INTERCHANGED DOUBLE CLOTHS

Two cloths may interchange vertically, producing a vertical stripe, or horizontally to produce a horizontal stripe. A cloth interchange in both directions therefore forms a square shape (the smallest unit being two ends and two picks). Because each cloth becomes a face cloth in turn (see page 100) the two layers are of equal importance, and this affects the choice of yarns and setting of the cloths.

Vertical cloth interchange

The illustration left shows the design effect of an example of a vertical interchange, between light and dark fabrics. Each stripe has eight ends – four to each cloth. Both cloths are plain weave, the ratio of ends and picks being one to one. 'Pockets' are formed between each interchange.

The sequence of cloth construction is as follows:
1 Draw out the weave construction of each cloth.
2 Establish the position of light and dark threads within the repeat unit (the warping and picking orders are not affected by the interchange). Draw a line at the point of intersection.
3 Mark the back ends and picks with a light tone. At this interchange line the face ends will become back ends, and the face picks back picks, and vice versa.
4 All face ends are lifted when the back pick is inserted. Record the lifted ends.
5 Enter the face-cloth weave where a face end crosses a face pick.
6 Enter the back-cloth weave where a back end crosses a back pick.
7 Reduce the weave notation to basic symbols.
8 Establish the draft. When the ends interchange their lifting sequence changes, and they must be entered on a separate group of shafts. Therefore eight shafts are required for this cloth construction.

The cloth interchange can be confined to weft only (as shown in the illustration left), or warp only, but though these affect the cloth's colour they do not interchange the cloths fully.

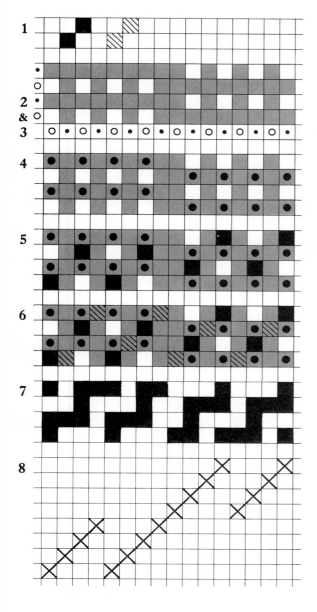

Construction sequence for a cloth with a vertical interchange.

Horizontal cloth interchange

In a horizontal interchange the weave constructions and end-to-pick ratio are the same as the example for vertical interchange. But because the interchange takes place horizontally, four ends form the warp repeat unit, while the picking plan has two repeat units of four picks each. As this cloth construction only requires four shafts it is within the scope of a four-shaft counterbalanced loom – providing each pedal is tied to a separate lam.

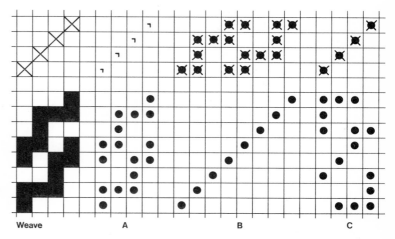

Horizontal cloth interchange:
A Lifting plan for a dobby or table loom
B Tie-up and pedalling sequence for a countermarch loom
C Tie-up and pedalling sequence for a counterbalanced loom

FULLY INTERCHANGED DOUBLE CLOTHS (DOUBLE PLAIN)

Fabrics constructed with both a vertical and a horizontal interchange are usually known as 'double plain' because both cloths are plain weave. (With more complicated weave constructions the number of shafts involved is quickly beyond the scope of most hand looms.) The end-and-pick ratio of one cloth to the other is generally one to one.

109

The construction sequence of a fully interchanged double cloth that can be divided into three design units. Both cloths are plain weave, and the face-to-back ratio of ends and picks is one to one.

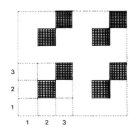

Four ends and four picks make up the repeat unit. A vertical cloth interchange requires eight shafts and four different pick intersections, while a horizontal interchange requires four shafts and eight different pick intersections (eight pedals for countermarch). Therefore a vertical and horizontal interchange needs eight shafts and eight pedals (for countermarch) for each design unit within the repeat.

An interchanged double cloth that can be divided into three design units is illustrated. Although each unit represents four ends and four picks, they can be numbered to find the draft and picking plan.

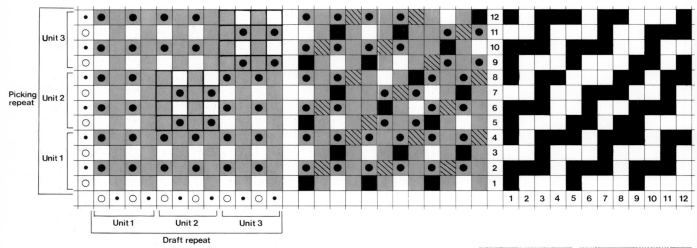

(*right*) The design units can be extended vertically or horizontally.

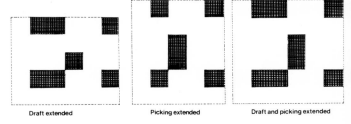

Draft extended   Picking extended   Draft and picking extended

The size of each unit can be changed by extending or rearranging the draft or lifting plan. And by placing draft units and picking units in different orders, more complex designs are possible as in this example (see opposite). The draft and weave construction of each unit are shown.

110

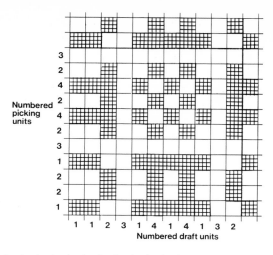

Numbered picking units

Numbered draft units

3 2 4 2 4 2 3 1 2 2 1

1 1 2 3 1 4 1 4 1 3 2

More complex designs can be made by placing draft units and picking units in different orders. This example has four design units and therefore requires sixteen shafts.
(*below*) The draft and weave constructions of each unit.

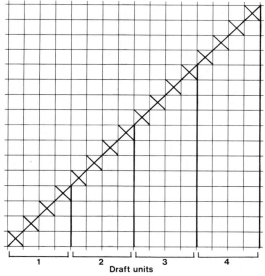

Draft units
1 2 3 4

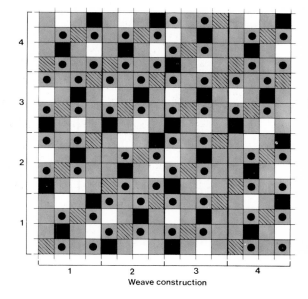

Weave construction
1 2 3 4

The method of constructing a fully interchanged double cloth is the same whatever the ratio of ends and picks of one cloth layer to the other. The example illustrated has a ratio of one to three ends and picks. There are also two different weaves; the light cloth being a plain weave construction, the dark cloth a more densely set $\frac{2}{2}$ twill. Six shafts are necessary for one repeat, two for the plain weave and four for the twill – therefore twelve are required to interchange the cloth.

A more interesting fabric can be made by interchanging two cloth layers of different density and construction.
(*below*) The design and cloth construction sequence.
(*below left*) The cloth construction.

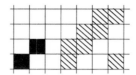

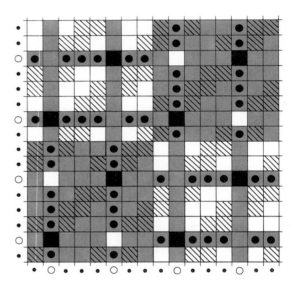

(*below*)
A Light cloth on the face
B Weft-only interchange
C Warp-only interchange
D Complete interchange

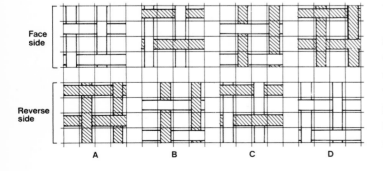

Face side

Reverse side

A   B   C   D

Warp-only and weft-only interchanges are possible as well as complete vertical and horizontal ones. The small design illustrates how the four alternatives can be used together: light cloth on the face, dark cloth on the face, weft interchange, warp interchange.

For a finely detailed or linear pattern the ends and picks of two plain-weave cloths can be interchanged in half units. The design should be divided into the total number of 'half units'. In the example illustrated opposite each square represents one half unit, and each half unit has two ends and picks. There are eight half units in the repeat, therefore sixteen shafts are required, and

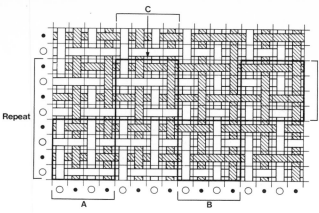

sixteen pedals on a countermarch loom. In each cloth the plain weave continues unbroken from one half unit to the next, though the two cloths are interchanged. And care must be taken to preserve the order of intersections across the width and length of the repeat (see illustration below). Because there are only two ends and picks in a half unit, two half units make a repeat, and the design repeat must be based on multiples of four ends and picks.

(*above and right*) Design using a combination of the four types of interchange.

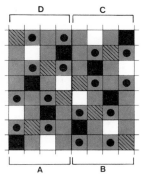

(*below*) A linear pattern where the ends and picks of two plain-weave cloths interchange within single ends and picks. Each vertical line of squares represents one face and one back end, each horizontal line represents one face and one back pick.

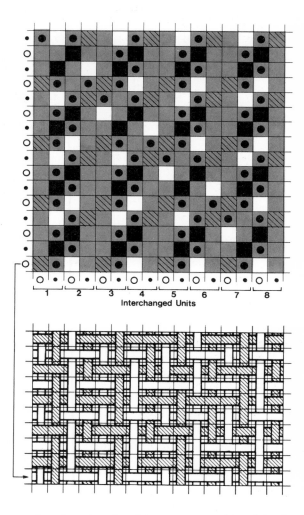

Care must be taken that the plain weave runs through both cloths unbroken. The design repeat must therefore be divisible by four.

113

A double plain cloth, the interchanges forming a shaded herringbone design. The dark cloth is made of a finer yarn and has twice as many ends and picks as the light. Sixteen shafts are required. Photos: John Hunnex

FREELY SELECTED DOUBLE PLAIN WEAVING

This technique is used mainly in Scandinavia where it is said to have originated. Within the limitations of a fully interchanged plain weave construction, it affords the weaver full creative freedom. The selection of the cloth layers to be interchanged is done by hand, without the aid of the draft or a complex lifting plan. The design can extend over the full warp width and its length is unlimited. These double cloths may be of any weight or quality, and they do not necessarily have to be square set. Once the technique is understood it lends itself to many variations.

Because this technique requires a hand selection of the interchanging cloth areas it cannot be woven on a power loom. Looms with a rising shed, such as table and dobby looms, lend themselves to this technique, but it is necessary to fix an angled bracket to the floor to hold down the pedal of a dobby loom while the design is picked out. Place the bracket close to the pedal in front of the foot position.

Looms with a centre shed, the countermarch and counterbalanced looms, do not need a pedal bracket but require the insertion of an additional stick (see method below).

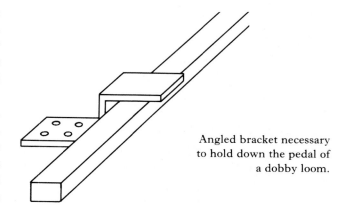

Angled bracket necessary to hold down the pedal of a dobby loom.

114

Whichever type of loom is used, to get a good shed the fell of the cloth should lie some distance from the reed.

Preparing the design

The first experiment is best done in contrasting colours. Draw the design on squared paper, each square represents half a repeat unit of a double plain-weave cloth, i.e. two ends plus two picks (see page 112); in the cloth illustrated both layers have identical setting. Thus if a design has 52 squares, the warp will require 104 ends. It is advisable to number the squares to assist the selection of the interchanging units.

The design drawn on squared paper, each square represents two ends and two picks, one of each cloth.

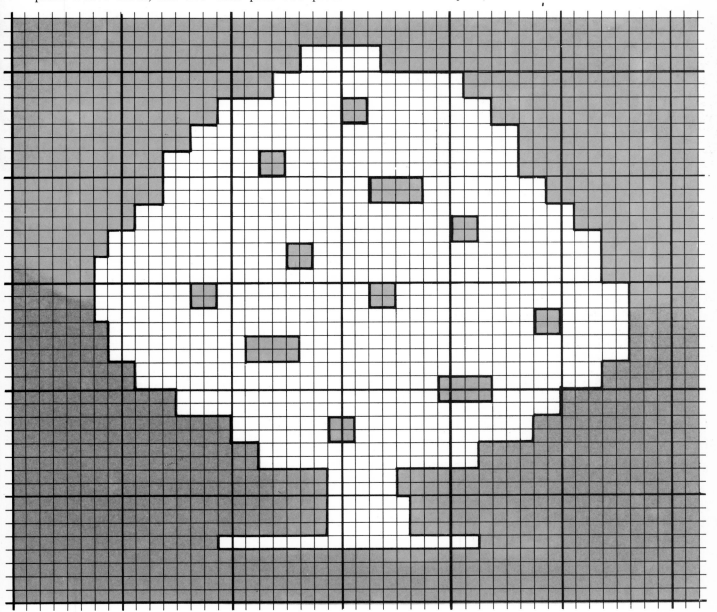

The cloth: face (opposite) and reverse (right). Photos: John Hunnex

Follow the numbered design pick by pick for the area selected. Remember that each group of units starts with a brown end and finishes with a white end.

The pattern illustrated has the following construction:

Warping plan:
2/10 Y.sk. (see Yarn Calculations page 13), brown, 1 end = draft symbol dark cross; 2/8 Y.sk., white, 1 end = draft symbol light cross.

Draft:
straight 1 to 4

Reed:
32 × 2 giving 64 ends per dm (8 × 2 giving 16 ends per in).

Weaving method on a table loom

A weave section is illustrated covering twenty ends and four picks. The sequence of actions to weave this section with a brown ground and a white motif is as follows:

First pick: white weft

1 Raise all brown ends by lifting shafts one and three.

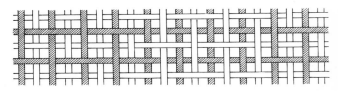

A weave section.

Brown warp ▥

White warp ○

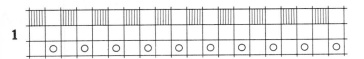

1

2 Insert a flat stick in front of the reed, below all brown ends that form the brown area of the design and above the brown ends which will lie below the white area of the design.

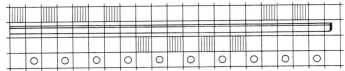

2

3 Drop the shafts.

4 Turn this stick on to its narrow side and hold it against the reed.

5 Insert a second stick in an identical position behind the reed.

6 Remove the first stick.

7 Make the first plain-weave shed of the white warp by lifting shaft two.

8 Insert the white pick.

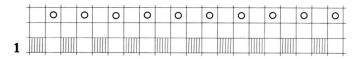

9 Beat down the weft.

10 Drop the shaft and withdraw the stick.

Second pick: brown weft

1 Lift all white ends by lifting shafts two and four.

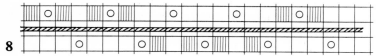

2 Insert the flat stick in front of the reed, below all white ends that form the white area of the design and above those that will lie below the brown area of the design.

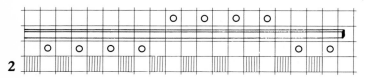

3 to **6** Proceed as for first (white) pick.

7 Lift the first brown plain-weave shed by lifting shaft one.

8 Insert the brown pick.

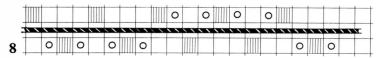

9 Beat down the weft.

10 Drop the shaft and withdraw the stick.

118

Third pick: white weft
Proceed as for the first pick, but make the second white plain-weave shed by lifting shaft four.
Fourth pick: brown weft
Proceed as for second pick, but make the second brown plain-weave shed by lifting shaft three.
Areas of solid colour across the width of the cloth are woven like ordinary double plain cloths (see page 109).

Weaving method on a dobby loom

When a dobby loom is used for this weaving technique, ten lags are pegged: six for the pick-up area and four for the double-plain ground. By skipping the unwanted lifts, the weaver has complete design freedom.

The time taken picking up the design can be halved if the two picks belonging to one colour group are woven consecutively: i.e. two white picks by lifting shaft two followed by four (before removing the sticks); two brown picks by lifting shaft one and then three. This method of weaving makes a coarser form of stepping in the design, which is further emphasized if the white and the brown ends are also grouped in twos in the warping plan and draft.

Weaving method on a countermarch loom

The weave is tied up on six pedals. Contrary to the normal procedure (see page 58), the first four pedals each allow a pair of shafts to float. To clarify the tie-up the following symbols are used:

▨ For shaft raised: cord from lower lam to pedal (as in normal tie-up).

☐ For shaft lowered: cord from upper lam to pedal (as in normal tie-up).

○ No lam-to-pedal tie-up. The shafts remain in the centre. The pedal tie-up is illustrated. To weave the same four picks of the pattern woven on the table loom, follow this procedure:

1 Press down pedal five, lifting all brown ends.
2 Insert flat stick in front of the reed under all brown ends that form the brown area of the design.
3 Release pedal five.
4 Turn flat stick on to the narrow side; press it against the reed.
5 Insert a round stick in the same shed opening behind the reed. (A round stick makes a clearer division.)
6 Remove the flat stick.
7 Press down pedal six, lifting all white ends.
8 Insert second stick, also round, behind the reed below all white ends and above brown ends not raised by the first stick insertion.
9 Release pedal six.
10 Press down pedal three which raises alternate white ends.
11 Pass the white weft through the shed.
12 Beat down the pick.
13 Remove all sticks.
For the three subsequent picks the procedure is exactly the same, but other pedals are used.

Second pick:
at **1** pedal six, at **7** pedal five, at **10** pedal one.
Third pick:
at **1** pedal five, at **7** pedal six, at **10** pedal four.
Fourth pick:
at **1** pedal six, at **7** pedal five, at **10** two.

To weave a solid brown ground four extra pedals have to be tied up (i.e. seven to ten).

Weaving method on a counterbalanced loom

The pedals are tied up one to a lam, so that the pedalling selection is free (see page 57). The pedalling plan is identical to the table loom, but the lifting plan is in reverse because the pedals pull the shafts down. The extra round stick inserted to get a clear shed in the countermarch loom is also necessary here.

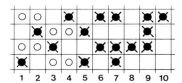

1 2 3 4 5 6 7 8 9 10

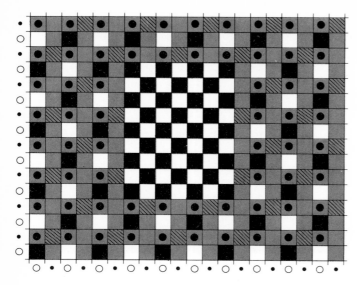

This form of weave combination can be used to achieve a wide range of quilted effects, and is successful with any weight of cloth.

A tubular cloth is usually formed from plain weave as this gives an unbroken surface; with a more complicated construction it is difficult to maintain the continuity of the weave.

DOUBLE AND SINGLE CLOTH COMBINED

All forms of double cloths can be combined with single cloths. The area of single cloth will have a much closer construction than the double (see illustration) unless a very loose weave is chosen. If the single cloth is firmly constructed it will distort the double cloth by straining outward toward the looser cloths.

TUBULAR CLOTHS

To form a woven tube, two identical cloth layers are joined at either side by the weft which passes alternately through the top and bottom shed making a continuous circle. There are no selvage ends. The weft tension must be carefully controlled to avoid pulling the warp in at either side and causing the density of the outer ends to increase. Care must also be taken with the cloth construction so that the weave continues correctly round the circumference of the tube. When a plain weave construction is used, the total number of ends in the warp must be based on an uneven number. The illustration shows a cross section through a tubular plain-weave cloth, with lifting plan. The draft is straight on four shafts.

A tubular cloth can be woven into a variety of diminishing shapes by reducing the ends gradually on one or both sides of the warp. The discarded ends are woven into the cloth before they are trimmed off, or left to form fringes. The width of the tube can also be changed at intervals by using wefts of different elasticity or varying shrinking properties.

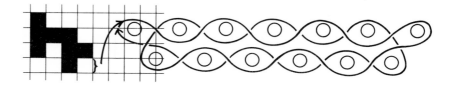

TREBLE CLOTHS

Three cloth layers may be combined in a number of ways, either for practical reasons or for the design opportunities they provide. Interesting fabrics can be made by interchanging cloths of varying colour and texture, but as each cloth requires a separate set of shafts their weave constructions are limited. When all three cloths are of plain weave construction the number of shafts per unit is six. The full design scope of three interchanging cloths can only be exploited on a jacquard loom.

The rules for constructing a treble cloth are the same as for the basic double cloth. Since there is an additional set of ends and picks two more symbols are required for the weave notation (see key to illustration, page 103).

An example of a treble cloth seen from the face and reverse sides; part of the top and centre layers have been removed to show each cloth.

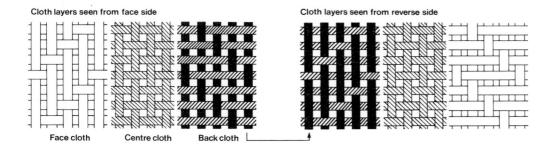

Cloth layers seen from face side

Cloth layers seen from reverse side

Face cloth   Centre cloth   Back cloth

The cloth construction is as follows:
1 Draw out the construction of the three cloths.
2 Mark the lines of squares allocated to the centre and back cloths. It is also advisable to mark the face, centre, and back ends and picks with 'F', 'C', and 'B' along the margins of the weave notation, to keep track of their position.

Treble-cloth construction sequence.

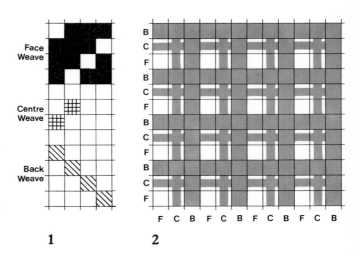

3 When the centre pick is inserted, all face ends are lifted, and when the back pick is inserted, all face and centre ends are lifted. Mark the lifting points accordingly.

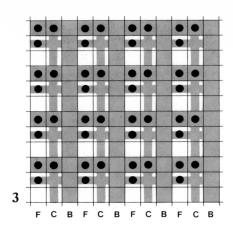

4 Allocate the three weave constructions to the appropriate lines of squares.

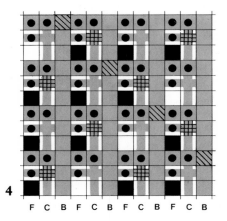

5 Reduce the weave notation to basic symbols and establish the draft by numbering.
Three unattached cloth layers can now be woven.

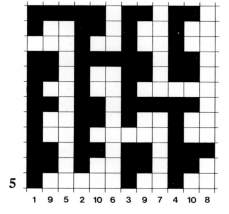

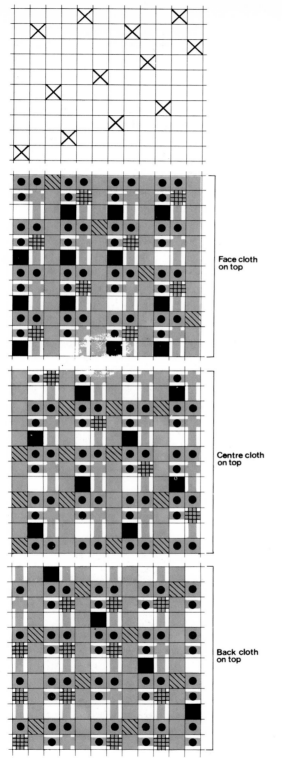

Face cloth
on top

Centre cloth
on top

Back cloth
on top

The cloths can be interchanged horizontally in any sequence with the same draft and picking order (see illustration left). To make a vertical or vertical and horizontal interchange of each cloth, i.e. so that each in turn becomes face, centre and bottom cloth would require thirty shafts – three groups of ten.

If there is no cloth interchange the layers can be held together by the centre cloth (see illustration below). The first centre end stitches into the face cloth, the third stitches into the back cloth. To do this the first and third ends of the centre cloth must be entered on separate shafts.

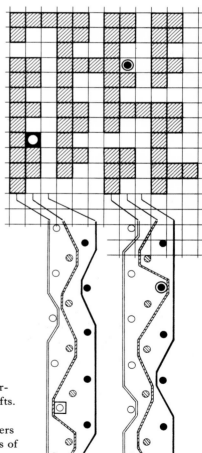

(*left*) Horizontal interchange using ten shafts.

(*right*) The three layers held together by ends of the centre cloth.

123

EXTENDED CLOTHS

Two or more layers of identical cloths may be joined on alternate sides during weaving by a single weft crossing from layer to layer. When the pick has been placed in the bottom layer, the shed is changed for the shuttle's return run. The passage of the shuttle thus follows a zigzag course, through the cloth layers. A double- and treble-layer cloth are illustrated. A double-layer cloth when unfolded will be of double width. The total number of ends in the warp must be divisible by four, as the weave must progress unbroken through the width of the cloth. A treble cloth will unfold to three times the weaving width. The total number of ends in the warp must be divisible by six.

In theory, any width of cloth can be woven by this method, but in practice this proves to be impossible because each layer requires a set of ends. The density of the warp is thus increased with every layer of cloth added and will reach a point when a shed formation becomes impossible.

SUPERIMPOSED CLOTH LAYERS

Instead of joining several layers of cloth at the side of the warp, they can be attached to each other at any point within the warp width. Each cloth forms a separate layer, is woven with a separate weft, and has selvages. The only point of attachment is a vertical line of interweaving. The width of the layers can be narrowed successively to form a superimposed ribbon effect (see colour illustration on page 102).

PLEATED FABRICS

Horizontal pleats can be incorporated in a fabric. The cloth construction has traditionally been limited to a basic weave – plain weave, twill, satin or sateen – but need not be confined to these. The cloth weight is best kept light. The size of the pleats is not restricted, nor is their distance from each other – except by the limitation of the number of lags in a dobby loom.

The warp must be divided into the ends which are in the ground cloth only and those that are both in the ground cloth and form the pleat. They are run off separate beams. The extra length of warp required for the pleat is calculated on the basis of the pleat size and the frequency of its occurrence.

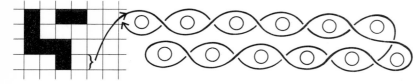

Double-layer extended cloth.

Treble-layer extended cloth.

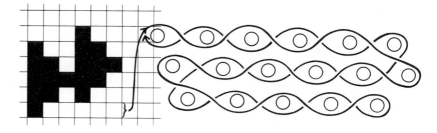

(*opposite*) Pleats spaced at irregular intervals. In this cloth both ground and pleats are plain weave, but they need not be of identical construction. Photo: John Hunnex

While the area which will form the pleat is woven, the ends that will hold the pleat formation are left floating at the back (see illustration). When twice the length of the pleat has been woven the pleat-cloth ends are relaxed sufficiently to allow the pleat to be brought forward by the reed, to the fell of the cloth. The next pick's intersection involves the ends of both warps (see illustration) and holds the pleat in position – providing the ground cloth is firmly constructed.

Pleated cloths can be woven on four shafts and without weaving problems. The difficulty arises in keeping a perfect warp-tension control. When a loom with a fixed tension control is used, the weaver must release sufficient warp for each pleat by lifting the pawl that controls the ratchet wheel (see page 20). With a friction-brake tension, the friction-controlling weight may be temporarily raised by a cord the weaver can operate from the front of the loom (see page 22), by which the weights can be lifted. The pleats can be spaced at any distance from each other.

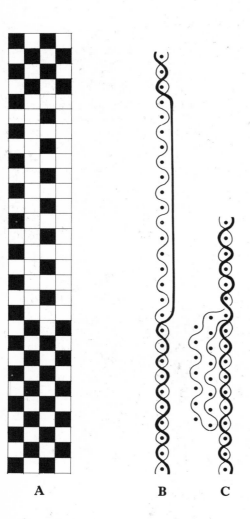

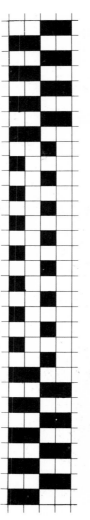

(*far left*)
A The weave
B The float end before beating up
C The pleat formation

(*left*) When two ends run together to form the ground weave, the ground cloth will be more firmly woven.

A   B   C

(*opposite*) Warp fringe fabric composed of a printed acetate warp and cotton weft. There is an equal proportion of ground and fringe ends. The warp floats were cut at the point where they re-enter the ground weave, after the cloth was taken from the loom. Fabric designed and woven by Kay Cosserat.

8 Pile fabrics

A pile is formed by ends or picks rising above the surface of the ground cloth. The pile may be loops or cut loops and whether it stands up or lies more or less flat largely depends on its density and height.

The quality of the cloth and the character of the pile depend as much on the nature of the yarns as on the setting and weave construction. For a strong, upstanding pile, a firm two-ply yarn must be used. Soft yarns – single or two-ply – will form a soft, flat pile. Continuous-filament yarns, particularly silk make beautiful pile fabrics. Yarns spun from short fibres and with little twist are unsuitable.

All pile fabrics must have a firmly constructed ground cloth, usually a plain weave or hopsack, into which the pile threads can be securely stitched. A very wide variety of pile fabrics can be made, covering the whole range of cloth weights – the densest and heaviest being a carpet, the lightest a fine velvet.

WARP PILE FABRICS

The best-known warp pile fabrics are velvets and moquettes. They require a minimum of two warps, one for the ground cloth, the other for the pile. A friction-brake tension is required to control the warp tension adequately. Only ends that make a pile of the same height and density, whether cut or uncut, can be placed on the same

(*opposite*) Looped weft pile formed by several threads of different colour and character grouped together, while the ground picks consist of single threads. A mixture of woollen and worsted spun yarns have been used.

beam. And if the degree of yarn take-up varies from end to end, each one must be drawn off a separate bobbin instead of a beam. The pile may cover the ground cloth completely, or be distributed in groups over the width of the warp.

To form the loops, the pile ends are lifted by a strip of flat wire placed in the shed instead of a

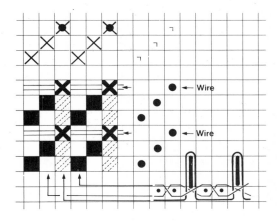

A warp-pile cloth construction with two ground ends to one pile end, and two ground picks between the loop formation. The pile ends are held in place by the density of the ground pick.

pick. Standing on its narrow edge, the wire is brought forward to the fell of the cloth, and held in position by one, two or more successive ground picks, very firmly beaten down. The height of the pile depends on the size of the wire; it can vary from a few millimetres to about 2·5 cm (1 in). Several wires have to be woven into the cloth before the first one can be withdrawn and used again to form the next loop.

To cut the loops, one end of the wire carries a knife, which cuts the loops as the wire is withdrawn. Alternatively, the cutting knife is supported over the wire, and guided by a V-shaped groove that runs through the wire's upper edge.

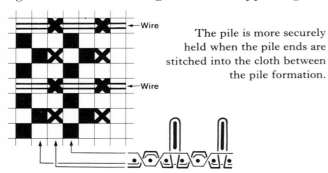

The pile is more securely held when the pile ends are stitched into the cloth between the pile formation.

Several wires must be woven into the cloth before the first one is withdrawn and reinserted.

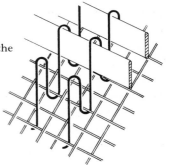

Terry towelling cloths

These nearly always have a looped pile on both sides. The density of the pile distribution varies considerably and affects the cloth's quality. The construction of a terry cloth is usually based on a ratio of one ground-cloth end to one pile end, and the position of the pile ends alternates from front to back. No wires are inserted; instead three picks are placed a little distance from the fell of the cloth and beaten down together while the beam carrying the pile warp is released. It is a weaving technique more easily carried out on the power loom, where the warp-tension control can be linked to the weaving cycle and the reed position changed mechanically.

Terry towelling cloths have a looped pile on both sides, formed usually by placing three picks at a distance from the cloth fell, and beating them down together while the pile warp tension is released. The distance between the woven groups of piles controls the pile height.

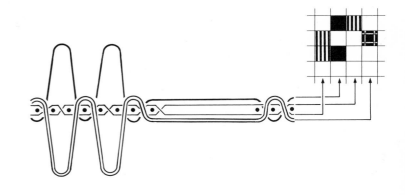

130

Warp fringe fabrics

These have loose ends hanging in horizontal stripes over the ground fabric (see colour illustration on page 127). The length can be varied from stripe to stripe. The fringe is formed by cutting floats of ends that have been stretched over a length of the ground cloth during weaving. It is important to weave the ends well in between fringes so that they are firmly secured. The fringe may be formed by alternate sets of ends, and may vary in density. Only one beam is required.

The fringe can either be cut as weaving progresses – before the cloth turns under the front bar – or when the fabric is complete. So that the fringe lies flat on the cloth roller, the warp floats should be cut as close as possible to the stitching point, with the fringe facing toward the reed. Hold the cloth taut while cutting the fringe ends if this is done after the cloth has been taken off the loom.

The character of the fringe depends on the density of its setting and on the nature of the yarn used to form it. For example, a smooth straight yarn will hang very straight, whereas a woollen yarn will contract and form a slightly curly fringe. The colour of the fringe yarn will affect the colour of the ground cloth.

WEFT PILE FABRICS

These fabrics need only one beam and the problem of a special warp-tension control, so important in warp pile fabrics, does not arise. On the other hand the number of shafts required is usually greater.

Weft loops have to be pulled up by hand. Both ground and loop picks follow a plain-weave sequence. Insert the loop pick with the shuttle. When it has reached the other side of the warp, place it so that extra lengths of yarn can easily be pulled off the bobbin. Keep the shed slightly open, and starting at the opposite side to the shuttle, pull up the loops with a shortened knitting needle set in a handle. Pull each loop up and forward to the fell of the cloth, secure it as firmly as possible

between the ends before the next loop is formed. The loops can be pulled up at any point and may vary in length. At least two ground picks should be placed between the loop picks. When loops of identical size are required, hold them on one or more knitting needles (depending on the width of the warp and the design distribution) while the ground picks are woven in.

To form a full rich loop pile, the yarn used for the pile pick should be soft and thick. It may also be made of several fine single threads run together (see colour illustration on page 128).

Weft fringe fabrics

The most commonly known cut weft pile fabric is corduroy. Cloths based on the corduroy weave construction have a firm base cloth and securely interwoven weft floats, which are subsequently cut. The pile forms vertical cords, their prominence depending on the density of the pile picks in relation to the ground cloth.

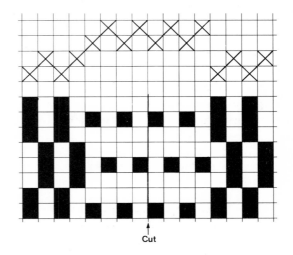

The floating picks should be cut at a point equidistant from the stitching lines.

131

A flatter, fringed stripe is made by keeping the ground-pick-to-pile-pick ratio at two to one, or even one to one and using a coarser ground pick. When the fringe extends beyond a certain length, it will droop. If two lines of stitching are used for the pile picks within the weave repeat unit, the position of the weft floats can be alternated (see illustration). This will make an overlapping pile fabric that has no stripe, but is not as completely directionless as velveteen, which requires more than two alternate stitching points.

A ground-to-pile-pick ratio of two to one makes a flatter, fringed stripe.

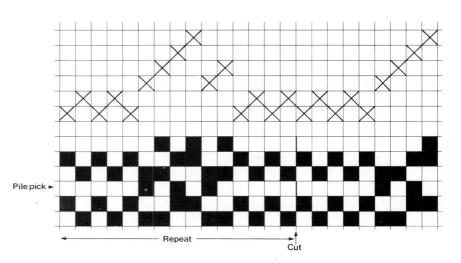

Alternating the position of the weft floats makes an overlapping pile fabric. The arrows indicate the points at which the floats are cut.

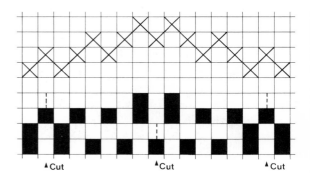

The hand weaver must cut the floats by hand, preferably in the loom when the fabric is taut. If the floats are too short to allow the insertion of a wire loop to support and guide the cutting knife it is best to use a pair of long, narrow hairdressers' scissors.*

Diagonal weft fringe fabrics

These are made in the same manner as fabrics with a vertical pile. The angle of the diagonal line is controlled by the weave construction and the density of the picks. The fringe droops if it is long. To make a significant diagonal stripe it is necessary to use at least twelve shafts.

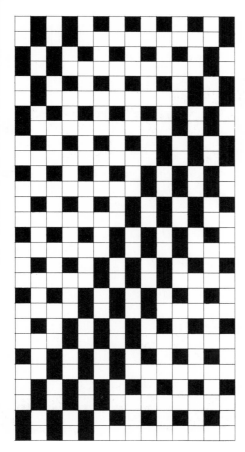

(below and left) At least twelve shafts are required for a diagonal weft pile. A fringe can be made by cutting the weft floats at the point where they interweave with the ground cloth.

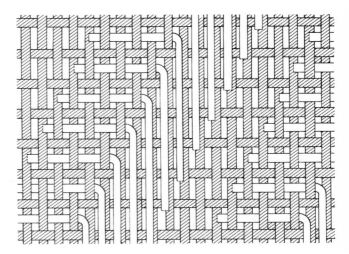

WARP AND WEFT PILE FABRICS (FRINGED SQUARES)

By combining the weave constructions of warp and weft cut pile fabrics fringed squares can be made. The centre of the square, where the pile ends and picks cross, may be woven as a double cloth (see page 103) or in some other looser weave construction (see illustration overleaf). Areas that form the fringe have double the number of ends and picks, i.e. they are crammed. When the squares are placed some distance apart, the pile threads would be too long if they were cut in the centre, and some of the yarn must be cut away. This can be done accurately by taking the floating threads to the back of the cloth at the point where they should be cut.

* Discussed and illustrated in 'The Technique of Rug Weaving' by Peter Collingwood, Faber 1968, 1969.

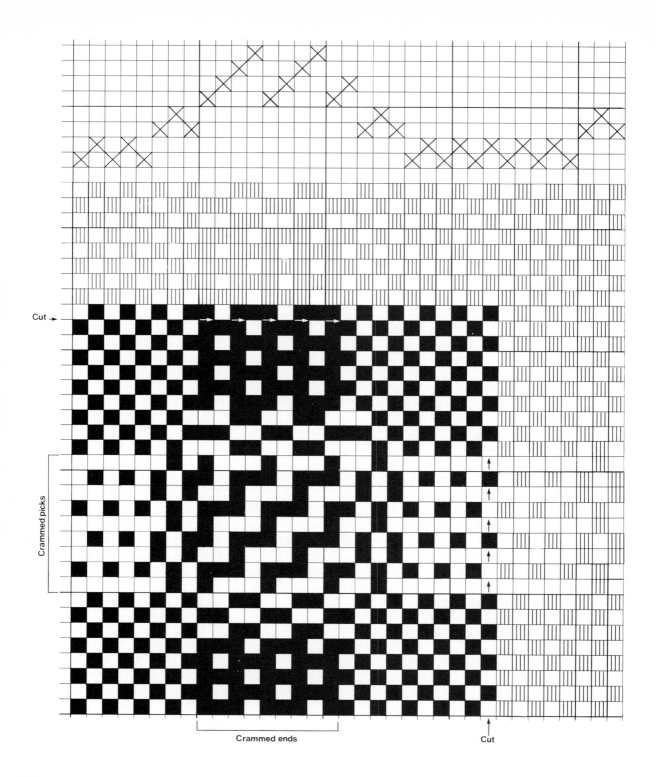

Cut →

Crammed picks

Crammed ends

Cut

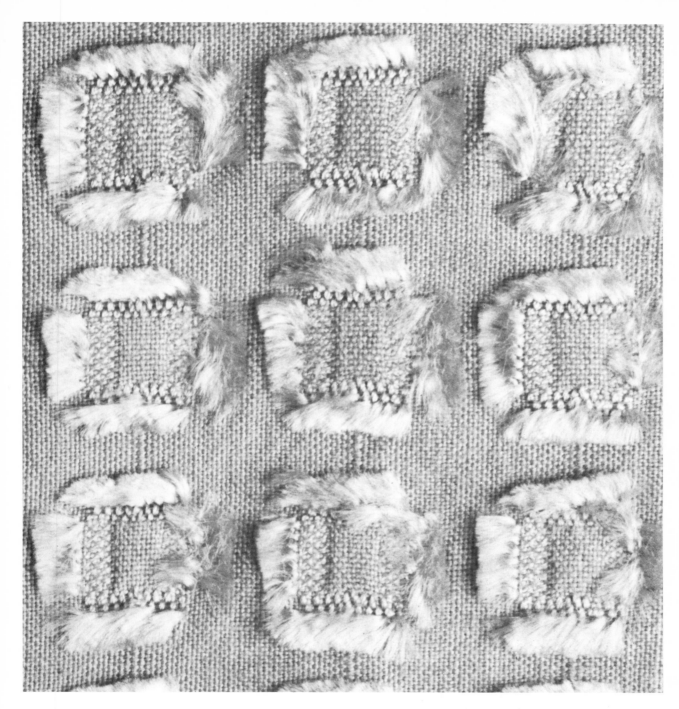

(*opposite*) Fringed squares. Take the floating ends to the back of the cloth at the point where they should be cut (arrowed).

(*above*) A cloth woven of worsted yarn with a warp and weft fringe, designed by Brenda Sparks. Photo: John Hunnex

135

9 Gauze and leno fabrics

The distinctive feature of these fabrics is that certain ends cross from side to side over/under one or more stationary ends, and are held in position by the weft. The crossing of the ends prevents the picks from packing closely together, yet at the same time holds them securely interwoven. Thus the fabrics formed have a light and open construction but they are also very stable.

Warp yarns for gauze and leno fabrics must be strong and smooth and free of knots.

The plain form of weaving with crossed ends is called gauze weave, all other forms of weaving with crossing ends that have a more complicated construction are called leno weaves.

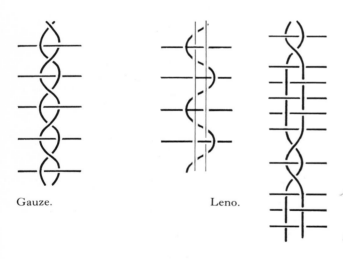

Gauze.   Leno.

The gauze weave repeat has a unit of two ends and two picks. This simple form of weaving with crossed ends is well within the scope of a countermarch, dobby or table loom. The shed formation does not present difficulties providing the appro-

priate doup shaft is added, and there is sufficient space between the front and back crossing shafts to allow the ends to cross without undue strain. The problem that does often baffle the hand weaver is how to control the warp tension.

Except for the gauze weaves, two beams are necessary. An easer bar in the form of a weighted rod should be placed over the crossing ends, and raised when the crossed shed is formed. On a dobby loom the easer bar can be attached to a spare hook that rises whenever the crossing shed is made. In a table loom the easer bar may be attached to the base of the loom by springs that are weak enough to allow the bar to rise when the crossing shed is made. The countermarch loom with its centre shed distributes the tension on the straight and crossing ends more evenly and makes an easer bar unnecessary, providing the warp yarn has some degree of elasticity.

GAUZE/LENO SHAFTS

In addition to the 'ordinary' shafts that carry the straight ends, three shafts are required to control the movement of each crossing end: a back crossing shaft (which is an ordinary shaft), a doup or half shaft, and a front crossing shaft (an ordinary shaft connected to the doup). The doup heddle passes through the eye and the shanks of the heddle of the ordinary shaft. Wire healds do not have divided shanks and are therefore difficult to use.

The doup shaft requires top and bottom sticks to suspend the shaft, although the doup heddle is only threaded to one. Both top and bottom doups can be used. Both are required for the countermarch loom because of its centre shed;

**Doup
heddle**

Gauze/leno shafts.

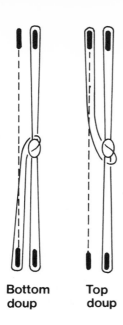

**Bottom
doup**

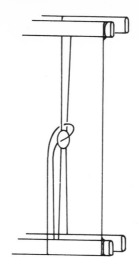

**Top
doup**

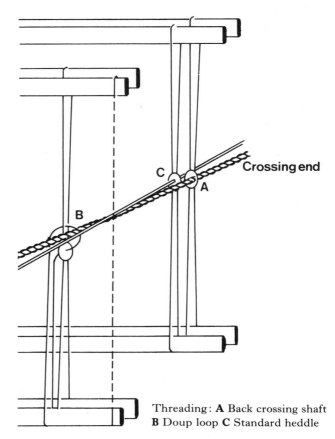

The doup shaft requires both top and bottom sticks to suspend the shaft from the shedding mechanism.

bottom doups only are used for the dobby and table looms which have rising sheds.

An industrial gauze/leno shaft consists of a pair of front crossing shafts with metal shanks in place of heddles. The shanks are connected by a bent needle with an eye in the bend.

Threading looms with a rising shed

The back crossing shaft takes the last shaft position, while the front crossing shaft/doup-heddle shaft unit is placed at the front. There should be a gap of no less than 10 cm (4 in) between the two to allow sufficient space for the ends to cross. The shafts for the straight ends are placed in this gap.

Thread the crossing end through the back crossing shaft (A), pass it under the straight end, and thread it through the doup loop (B). The doup loop may face either to the right or to the left. If it faces to the right, the back crossing heddle lies to the right of the standard heddle (C); when it faces to the left, the back crossing heddle lies to the left. The crossing end, and the end or ends under which it crosses, must always be entered in the same dent in the reed.

Threading: **A** Back crossing shaft **B** Doup loop **C** Standard heddle

When the back crossing shaft and the doup shaft are lifted, the doup heddle is extended and the crossing end passes under the straight end and rises. This is called an open shed because the ends do not cross. By raising both shafts of the front crossing shaft unit, the crossing end crosses under the straight end (see illustration below).

When industrial gauze/leno shafts are used, the crossing end is threaded through the back crossing shaft and the eye of the bent needle connecting the two front supporting shafts. The straight end passes between the shanks. To make the open shed, raise the second front shaft (2) and the back crossing shaft. To make the crossed shed, raise the first front shaft (1). These shafts can only be used in a dobby loom.

Industrial shafts.

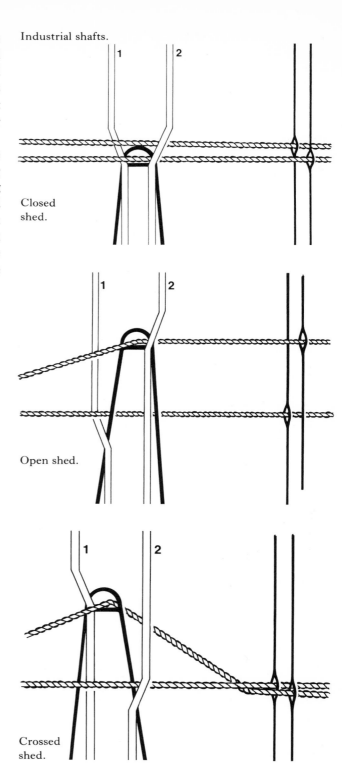

Closed shed.

Open shed.

Crossed shed.

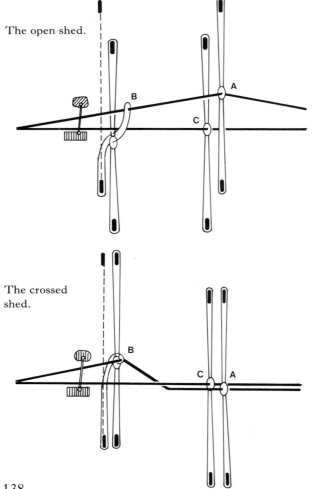

The open shed.

The crossed shed.

138

WEAVING ON A DOBBY LOOM

The lifting-plan notation is the same as for ordinary weaving. With industrial leno shafts, in plain gauze cloth the open and closed shed alternates. The straight end is not lifted itself, but interwoven by the pick that passes under each crossing end (see illustration right). To make the crossing ends cross in opposite directions, reverse the threading order of the back crossing shaft and the standard shaft.

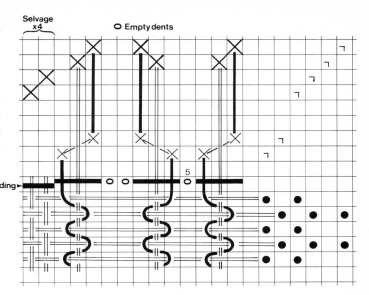

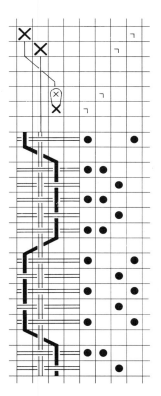

(*left*) Crossing threads with string doups and a supporting shaft. This is a leno variation in which the crossing end is held on alternate sides of the straight end by a number of plain-weave picks.

(*right*) A leno weave with more than one straight end requires extra shafts added in front of the back crossing shaft.

(*above*) With industrial shafts reverse the threading order of the back crossing shaft and standard shaft to make the crossing ends cross in opposite directions.

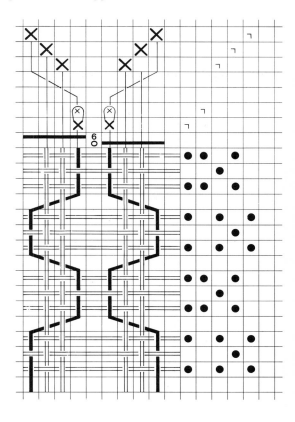

Weaving with string doups and a supporting shaft requires a different lifting plan, because the lifting of the front crossing unit is the equivalent of lifting two shafts (see illustration). To weave a leno fabric with more than one straight end, extra shafts are added in front of the back crossing shaft. Two sets of back and front crossing shafts

139

are required to alternate plain weave and leno weave in groups of ends. To form stripes of straight ends between gauze weave constructions, place extra shafts wherever it is most convenient between the front and back crossing shafts.

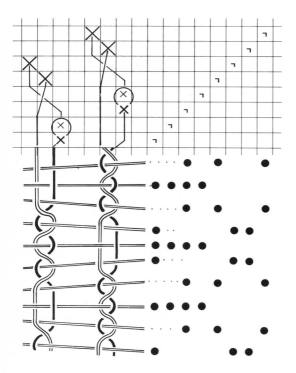

Alternating sequences of leno weave formations need two sets of back and front crossing shafts.

WEAVING ON A TABLE LOOM

On a table loom with a rising shed the lifting plan and weaving method are the same as are used for the dobby loom with string doup heddles.

WEAVING ON A COUNTERMARCH LOOM

Because this loom has a centre shed, the crossing and straight ends have to rise and fall. The tension on both groups of ends is therefore identical.

For a gauze weave no standard shaft is used; instead an additional back crossing shaft is required. The first doup shaft unit has a bottom doup placed in front of the supporting shaft. The second doup shaft unit has a top doup placed behind the supporting shaft. Thread the first end in the shafts from left to right (seen from the front of the loom). Thread it through the seventh shaft between the shanks and above the eye of the heddle, and then through the loop of the first doup shaft unit, facing to the left (see illustration). Thread the second end between the shanks of the eighth shaft below the heddle eye, cross it over the end already entered and thread it through the doup loop of the second doup shaft unit, facing to the right. Thus the two doups face each other. Two extra shafts (five and six) are added to carry ends not involved in the leno weave. The greater the distance between the back shaft and the doup shafts, the less strain is exerted on the crossing ends.

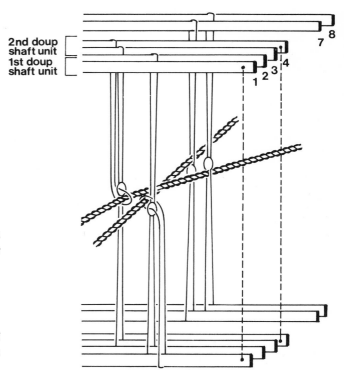

When weaving on a countermarch loom, an additional back crossing shaft replaces the standard shaft. More than two extra shafts may be carried for a more complex weave.

The three lifting positions of the front crossing shafts are illustrated. Raising the first crossing shaft unit and lowering the second forms the crossing shed (A). The back shafts remain in the neutral position. The open shed is formed by raising the first doup shaft (shaft 1) and the supporting shaft of the second doup shaft unit (shaft 3) while the second doup shaft (shaft 4) and the supporting shaft of the first doup shaft unit (shaft 2) are lowered (B). The seventh shaft is raised, the eighth lowered. To weave horizontal stripes of plain weave between gauze areas a third pedal is required which forms the alternate plain shed by lowering the first crossing unit and raising the second, while the back crossing shafts remain in the neutral position (C).

The draft, tying-up plan, pedalling sequence and resultant weave are illustrated. Because not all shafts move, they are not all connected to a pedal. This requires an additional symbol in the tying-up plan – a circle – to represent no tie to a pedal.

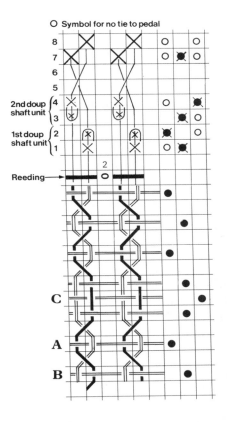

A gauze weave on a counter-march loom with more than one plain-weave intersection between crossing ends. Note the empty dents in the reeding plan. The shafts tend to drop a little when the jacks are released; this can be counteracted by weighting the upper lams with one or two pedals (see page 33).

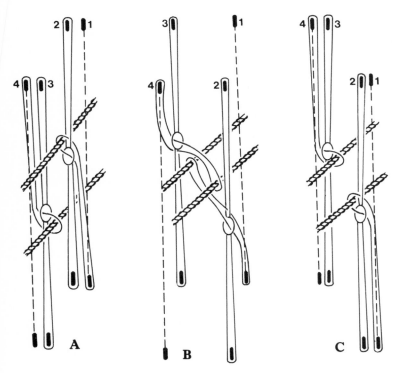

A Crossing shed   **B** Open shed   **C** Alternate open shed
The two plain-weave sheds, B and C, allow the crossing end to be woven first on one side of the straight end and then on the other.

141

10 Cloth finishing

The appearance and handle of many fabrics is not fully developed until they have undergone one or more finishing processes after removal from the loom. Cloth finishing can take many forms and requires specialist knowledge. A full account lies beyond the scope of this book, nor would the hand weaver have the facilities to cope with the majority of processes. Only those that can be carried out in workshop conditions are briefly discussed. A designer/weaver who submits woven prototypes to a manufacturer must acquire the necessary knowledge of industrial finishing processes in order to be able to take these into account while designing.

All fabrics should be carefully inspected as soon as they leave the loom. Before being submitted to a finishing treatment, all broken ends and weaving faults must be repaired, visible knots undone and their ends stitched into the cloth.

Silk fabrics require no after-treatment, except those made from spun silk. Press these when dry with a medium-hot iron to increase the lustre and softness of handle.

Cotton, linen, and synthetic fabrics do not generally require an after-treatment, unless a specific property such as crease resistance is required. But linen, and to a lesser extent cotton, fabrics shrink when washed for the first time, and should be pre-shrunk if the dimensional stability of the cloth is essential. The washing can be done by hand or machine and no special drying method is necessary. Both cotton and linen should be pressed damp with a very hot iron. Cotton on the reverse side; linen on the face side to give it maximum lustre. Synthetic fabrics mostly need a cooler iron as many are likely to melt if the heat is too great. By ironing the handle of the cloth is softened.

Cloths woven from clean oil-free wool or worsted, be they single, folded or effect yarns, do not necessarily require a wet finishing process. Upholstery or curtain fabrics, for example, are not subject to finishing unless for a specific purpose, such as to make them fireproof or anti-static. Softer fabrics woven for garments have to be given dimensional stability and a controlled elasticity to prevent bagging and thread slippage. They undergo a 'setting' process, which entails steaming the cloth: place the fabric between a pair of damp cloths, and press it with a very hot iron. The amount of steaming depends on the weight and character of the cloth. The iron must be lifted from position to position, not slid along the board as in ordinary ironing. Continue until all the steam has been absorbed by the heat. Care must be taken to ensure that the ends and picks lie at right angles to each other. To maintain the correct width over the whole length of the piece, mark the intended width of the cloth on the ironing board or table and keep the picks parallel to the edge.

When oil and dirt are present in woollen or worsted yarn, the cloth has to be 'scoured'. All wet finishing should be carried out in soft water and with pure soap or a good scouring agent.

A worsted cloth has to be set by steaming before it is scoured, to prevent fibre contraction and shrinkage while retaining the clear, non-fibrous surface of the cloth.

Woollen cloths are allowed greater shrinkage and fibre movement, they are not submitted to a setting process. Heavy, very oily cloths should be soaked in cold water for several hours before scouring; soak light and fine cloths for no more than an hour. Scour in soapy water at a temperature of 45–50°C (110–120°F), and use sufficient water for the cloth to be moved about and turned as it is squeezed. The cloth must not be rubbed nor wrung during the scouring process. Use two or more changes of soapy water at the same temperature until the cloth has no noticeable traces of oil but still retains the softness of handle. Detergents remove the oil so completely that the handle becomes harsh and 'dry'. Wash out all traces of soap by thorough rinsing. Surplus moisture can be removed either by spin drying, or by wrapping the cloth in a series of towels, or by pressure. The final drying is done on a stenter frame or on a slatted drying roller.

A drying roller should have a circumference of no less than 38 cm (15 in) and a length that will hold the widest cloth that can be woven on the loom(s) available. Wind the cloth on to the roller in a damp state, face inward. Place the starting end parallel to the wooden slats and hold it down under an extra slat, securing this at either end with adjustable cords. While the roller is slowly turned stroke the cloth in both directions with the palms of both hands, thus giving a degree of tension round the roller and across the width. The width must be kept constant and the picks parallel to the slats. The end of the cloth is held down in the same way. Stand the roller on end while the cloth is drying; its position should be occasionally reversed. If it is a long length of cloth rewind when the outer layers are dry, to bring the inner layers uppermost.

Cloths that require a greater degree of shrinkage have to be 'milled' after scouring. For this process prepare a good soap lather in the minimum of hot water. Squeeze all surplus water out of the cloth before placing it in a heap in the soap suds. Small quantities of cloth can be milled by pounding it with the fists in a basin or sink. Larger quantities are best treated by walking on them in the bottom of the bath, or by using a suction possing stick. Turn the cloth over continually during this process so that all parts get the same degree of treatment. The time taken to achieve the required shrinkage will vary considerably according to the quality of the wool fibre, the amount of twist in the yarn, and the weave construction. Frequent inspection of the cloth is therefore essential to prevent overmilling – a fault that cannot be corrected. Rinse the cloth thoroughly after milling and dry it on a roller. Milling gives the cloth a more fibrous surface. This can be further increased by brushing with a stiff brush.

A few firms of woollen finishers are willing to accept short, handwoven lengths for treatment; but individual treatment is thereby lost because pieces of varying width, weight, and character are joined together and summarily treated.

A drying roller.

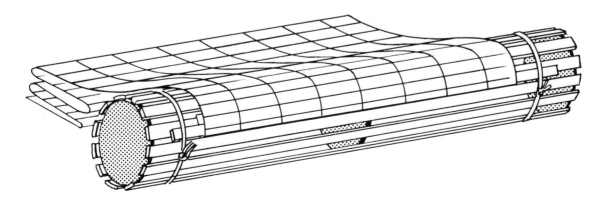

Appendix: worksheets and records

All information concerning the making of a cloth should be recorded on a worksheet before work begins. It should be stated in a simple, concise form.

If a design is evolved in the loom, any additional information must be added to the worksheet as work proceeds and alterations made at any stage of the preparatory or weaving processes must also be recorded. It is fatal to rely on memory.

When the job is completed, the worksheet becomes a record. It is the basis of any cost calculation, and can be referred to at any time should the same cloth have to be woven again. It also forms a very valuable reservoir of reference material.

If in doubt as to the amount of information required on a work/record sheet, it is useful to take the following criterion as a guide: anyone familiar with weaving should be able to produce an identical cloth by following the record without referring back to its originator. As to the layout of such information sheets, each weaver and textile manufacturer tends to evolve a system suitable to the type of cloth chiefly produced, but it is essential that sufficient space is allowed to accommodate all the information.

Complex point-paper notations should preferably be given in colours, not symbols. They are easier and quicker to understand. Warping and picking plans are written in a condensed form that shows at a glance how many yarn packages are required for the warp, and their arrangement in the creel.

Warping plan:

Example

Yarn (count/ref. no./col.)	2		1	1	1	1	=	6
Yarn (count/ref. no./col.)	1	2	2		1	1	=	7
Yarn (count/ref. no./col.)	1	1	1	2	1	1	=	7

ends per repeat = 20

The grid is read from top to bottom, starting on the left. A picking plan is written in the same way.

Example

4 ×

Yarn (count/ref. no./col.)	2	2	1	3	= 20
Yarn (count/ref. no./col.)	1		1	1	= 6
Yarn (count/ref. no./col.)		1		2	= 6

picks per repeat = 32

A SPECIMEN WORKSHEET

This sheet covers all general information required. Additional information may be needed for individual cloths.

For filing purposes a reference number or name is useful.

WARP
Yarn (ref. no.) .... *Count* ....
Colour (ref. no.) ....

If more than one yarn/colour is used record the warping plan.

If more than one warp is used for a fabric, separate details are required for each.
Width of warp: .... (including or excluding selvages)
Length of warp: ....
Total number of ends: ....

For vertical warping mill
Number of ends per portee: ....
Total number of portees: ....

For horizontal warping mill
Number of ends per section: ....
Total number of sections: ....

Reed:
Dents per measured unit (dents per dm/in): ....
Ends per dent: ....

If the reeding is irregular a reeding plan must be included.

Draft: ....

If the yarn/colour position is related to the draft or the reeding plan or both, the necessary information has to be included in the notation.

Pegging plan, lifting plan or pedal tie-up with pedalling sequence: ....

WEFT:
Yarn (ref. no.) .... *Count* ....
Colour (ref. no.) ....

If more than one weft is used, a picking plan must be added.

If the yarns/colour relate to specific picks, their position has to be included in the weaving instructions, pegging plan or any other form of lifting plan.

Picks per cm (in): ....

If the cloth has to undergo a finishing process give details of the process including the cloth's measurements: ....
Width of cloth: .... *before finishing*
.... *after finishing*
Length of cloth: .... *before finishing*
.... *after finishing*
Weight of cloth: .... *before finishing*
.... *after finishing*

Other useful information:
Weight of the warp: ....

If the cloth is not finished:
Width out of the loom (when the cloth is relaxed):
....

Picks per cm (in) (when the cloth is relaxed):
....

Knots used in hand weaving

It is essential that all knots used in tying up should hold firm while the loom is in use, but can easily be untied when necessary. For this reason it is important to use the correct knot in relation to its function in the loom. Knots in the yarn have to be as small as possible, yet must withstand both the tension of the warp and the friction of the reed.

1 *Knots used on the loom*
To prevent the cords used in tying up from fraying at the ends, dip them in a dilute varnish or liquid adhesive. When the varnish or adhesive is almost dry, roll the cord ends between finger and thumb to make them firm and as thin as possible.
Snitch knot: an easily adjustable knot, quick to untie, used to suspend shafts, attach lams to shafts and pedals to lams.
Single-cord snitch knot: a less easily adjustable knot used for shaft suspension.

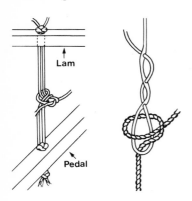

Single-cord spliced knot: easily adjustable, also used for shaft suspension.

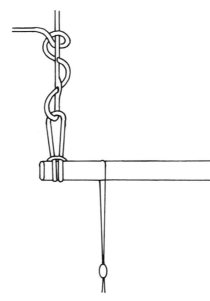

Single ring hitch: used to tie the portee and starting sticks to the apron stick.

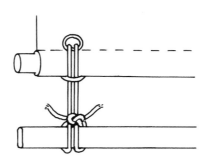

Double ring hitch: used whenever a very firm grip is required,

for example to hold the shafts of a counterbalanced loom immobile while tying up.

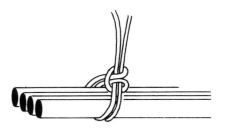

2 *Attaching the warp to the starting stick*
Commonly used method: the ends are tied with a reef (square) knot.

For fine, smooth yarns: where a reef (square) knot might slip open, tie groups of ends with an overhand (dog) knot and thread a cord through each group and round the starting stick.

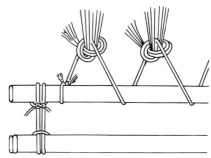

3 *Knots used to join two yarns*
Common weavers' knot:

A Place the 'light' thread over the 'dark' thread from left to right and hold the crossing between thumb and first finger of the left hand.

B Loop the dark thread up over the thumb and pass it behind itself and in front of the light thread. Pull it down between the thumb and first finger.

C Withdraw the thumb slightly to allow the end of the light thread to be bent down into the loop by either the first finger or thumb of the right hand.

D Hold both ends of the light thread with the thumb and close the knot by pulling the dark thread back.

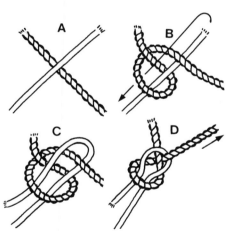

Double weavers' knot: used for smooth yarns, this is formed in the same way as the common weavers' knot, but at the second stage wind the dark thread once round the light thread.

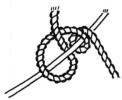

Half bow: when either a coarse or a fragile yarn is used in the warp it is advisable not to weave knotted ends through the shafts and reed. Knot a repaired end well back and tie an extra length of yarn in a half bow. This can be undone when the knot reaches the shafts to supply enough yarn for the knot to be pulled forward beyond the fell of the cloth.

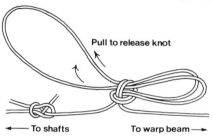

Pull to release knot

← To shafts   To warp beam →

Overhand (dog) knot: used to join fine yarns, e.g. silk.

Reef (square) knot: an alternative to the weavers' knot.

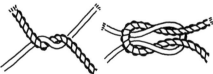

4 *Joining old and new warps*
When joining old and new warps sit between the pairs of cross sticks and work toward yourself.
Spanning-in knot: used to join ends at the correct tension when a new warp is tied to a finished one. The yarn tension is established at the third stage and locked by a half hitch round the old warp end.

It is also useful to span-in single ends that have broken at the back of the loom.

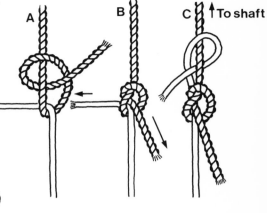

5 *Adjusting warp tension*
Slack can be taken up by twisting a group of ends round each other, and the twist secured by a pencil or peg. This can be done either near the starting stick before beginning to weave, or close to the warp beam during weaving.

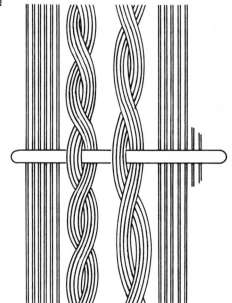

147

Further reading

Albers, Anni *On Designing* Middleton, Conn.: Wesleyan University Press 1975

Albers, Anni *On Weaving* London: Studio Vista 1974; Middleton, Conn.: Wesleyan University Press 1965

Blumenau, Lili *The Art and Craft of Hand Weaving* New York: Crown 1955

Emery, Irene *The Primary Structures of Fabrics* Washington: Textile Museum 1966

Hooper, Luther *Hand-Loom Weaving* London: Pitman 1920; New York: Pitman 1920

Kirby, Mary *Designing on the Loom* London: Studio 1955; Pacific Grove, Calif.: Select Books 1973

Marsh, J. T. *An Introduction to Textile Finishing* London: Chapman and Hall 1966

Miller, Edward *Textiles : Properties and Behaviour* London: Batsford 1973; Plainfield, N.J.: Textile Book Service 1973

Murphy, John *A Treatise on The Art of Weaving* London: Blackie 1857

Nisbet, Harry *Grammar of Textile Design* London: Scott Greenwood 1919; Plainfield, N.J.: Textile Book Service

Robinson, A. T. C. and Marks, R. *Woven Cloth Construction* Manchester: The Textile Institute 1973; Plainfield, N.J.: Textile Book Service 1973

The Textile Institute *Textile Terms and Definitions* Manchester: The Textile Institute 1975; Plainfield, N.J.: Textile Book Service 1975

The Textile Institute *The Identification of Textile Materials* Manchester: The Textile Institute 1976; Plainfield, N.J.: Textile Book Service 1976

Thorpe, A. S. and Larson, J. L. *Elements of Weaving* Garden City, N.Y.: Doubleday 1967

Watson, William *Textile Design and Colour* London: Newnes-Butterworth 1975; Plainfield, N.J.: Textile Book Service 1975

Watson, William *Advanced Textile Design* London: Longmans, Green 1965; Plainfield, N.J.: Textile Book Service 1975

Index